MOVES TO *make* AND PATHS TO *take*

FOR REAL ESTATE INVESTING SUCCESS

LANDLORD *by* DESIGN 2

Beachrock Publishing

beachrockpublishing.com

ISBN: 9780995303706 (paperback)
ISBN: 9780995303713 (ebook)
ISBN: 9780995303720 (audiobook)

Ordering Information:
Special discounts are available on quantity purchases by corporations, associations, and others. For details, contact info@landlordbydesign.com or visit landlordbydesign.com.

Disclaimer:
The publisher and the author do not make any guarantee or other promise as to any results that may be obtained from using the content of this book. You should never make any investment decision without first consulting with your own financial advisor and conducting your own research and due diligence. To the maximum extent permitted by law, the publisher and the author disclaim any and all liability in the event any information, commentary, analysis, opinions, advice and/or recommendations contained in this book prove to be inaccurate, incomplete or unreliable, or result in any investment or other losses.

LANDLORD *by* DESIGN 2

MICHAEL P. CURRIE

DEDICATION

To all those who suffer from real estate investing FOMO
and the crippling feeling that everyone can make money
in real estate except you

TABLE OF CONTENTS

PREFACE

I can't believe that there are any heights that can't be scaled by a man who knows the secrets of making dreams come true.

—WALT DISNEY

I T *was* A TUESDAY AROUND 8:30 P.M. WHEN I got the call. It had been a long day at work, and I was finally home, hanging out with my wife and two-year-old son. It felt good to be home relaxing, and I was warm and cozy in my comfy chair, eating chicken noodle soup when the phone rang.

This wasn't the first call I'd gotten about the building. It had only been a month and half since I'd purchased the property, and I was already getting calls nearly every day. It shouldn't have been a shock, but for some reason, on this particular night, it broke me. When I got off the phone, I said to my wife, "Why are these people ruining my life? Can't they just mind their business and live in peace?"

You see, I closed on this property on December 30 of the previous year, and the first calls came in December 31, New Year's Eve. They consisted of two drunken messages—one from my superintendent and one from a tenant. I listened as each shared their side of a story about loud music and a physical altercation between them, which had been broken up by other tenants in the building. The stage had been set, and basically every day after that, I would receive a call related to either a building maintenance issue or a problem with the tenants—like the kids who stole the fire extinguishers, and a few others who paintballed the front of the building.

Unfortunately, this call was more of the same.

A few reckless kids across the street broke one of the apartments' living room windows. I called my superintendent to join me in addressing the issue. When I arrived, the tenants were out in the street, eager to watch the confrontation.

I walked up to the culprit's house and told them to come outside so we could talk. They refused and stayed inside, cowardly threatening me with a baseball bat through the window. Fortunately, someone called the police so that a peaceful resolution could occur before I lashed out and started a fight I'd regret.

"It's not worth it. Step away," the officer said. This is the exact moment I became inducted into the ranks of a landlord.

While it wasn't easy, I learned a lot in those early days. The previous two years had been easy by comparison. I'd successfully purchased, renovated, and had great tenants in three other two-unit properties. This new property was my fourth in two years and was my first larger property consisting of six units. At the time I felt going after doors was the path to success and financial freedom. As things became more challenging, I had to adapt, change, and learn from others, and the lessons I learned led me to write about my experiences as a real estate investor.

I know many of you might be thinking, "Why continue is this line of work after having such a crazy experience?" Well, I did re-evaluate what real estate investing meant to me, what my long-term goals were, and how I was going to get there. At the time I figured these were simply growing pains, and I just needed to keep pushing if I wanted to reach my goals. It wasn't until a few years later that I changed my strategy and sold some of my problem properties. Twistedly enough, even when I sold these bad properties, I made money. I knew as I moved forward, I would have to come up with a plan that worked for me. I had to run my own race.

Keep in mind that everyone's landlord journey will be different. The business models are almost endless. Over the years, I've tried a variety of different real estate investing strategies, and it's my aim to share these experiences with you here so you can learn from my successes and failures. For those instances when my personal experience might not be enough, I've consulted with business associates with subject matter expertise to provide you with enough information to get a conversation started.

This simple, easy-to-read book will show you how to make money as a real estate investor immediately. Although I've had some ups and downs, real estate has provided a great subsidy to my family's income. It's close to free to participate, and you deliver a recession-proof product that never goes out of style.

The stories and ideas within are for those looking for additional income to subsidize their lifestyle. It can help you to cover the mortgage, tuition for a child's private school or university, make car payments, or pay for family vacations. This is for all those looking to become successful from real estate investments that will enhance your lifestyle and perhaps eventually lead to a portfolio to cover all your bills and retirement.

Whatever your dream is, big or small, real estate investing can provide it for you. So, let's start today, keep it simple, and learn how to use real estate investing as a tool to live the life you want to live on your terms.

It is my hope that this book inspires you to take action.

ONE

PROPERTY MANAGEMENT

I T WAS A *cold* SUNDAY IN FEBRUARY, MY first winter as a landlord and property manager. I received a call from a tenant saying that her furnace wasn't working. (As a side note, it always seems as if repairs are required at the most inconvenient times, like weekends or holidays.) I contacted my friend who owned a heating company, and though he was unavailable, he had an on-call employee who could get on-site in three hours. This didn't stop the tenant from contacting me four more times in the next three hours to ask when they were coming and to describe how cold it was getting in the house. Each time, I assured her someone would be there soon.

Since the house was heated with oil, when the furnace tech arrived, he had to bleed the system. As it turned out, the problem with the furnace started when the tenant let the tank run out of oil. When I asked the tenant, they feverishly denied the allegation. The furnace had been serviced just a few months prior, so I knew the tenant was not being truthful. However, I decided it would be best to not push the issue and to move on. The problem was solved, and just to make sure there were no issues in the future, I discussed the importance of keeping oil in the tank. I followed this up with a change in policy for future tenants that requires a minimum of a quarter tank. I also made sure to state that we charge a service fee for bleeding lines.

Unfortunately, these types of calls really got to me as a new landlord. While those feelings don't completely go away, with time, training, and experience, everyday problems become much easier to deal with. Since I have already written a book on property management, I'm not going to delve into that topic any further here. I will say that when you're starting out, self-manage at least your first few properties if possible. This will allow you to get hands-on property management experience that's invaluable. I can assure you this will make you a better client for future property managers you hire, save you money, and help you build the confidence and knowledge necessary to manage your portfolio.

So, what does it mean to manage properties? First and foremost, you need to set and collect the rent. You'll also need to organize and coordinate the residents, conduct maintenance and repair work, oversee the capital repair schedule, and pay all the bills (which can include water, electricity, gas, and internet). If you don't have a staff, you might also be a customer experience and service agent and, at times, a negotiator when you need to deal with emotionally charged tenants.

If you decide you want to hire a property manager, I would advise caution. For the most part, it's an unregulated occupation. The person you hire will have control of not only the revenue collection but also the actual asset. My intent is to absolutely scare you, as you will need to screen and hire a great property manager.

In the event that you hire a bad property manager, these are possible consequences:

Conducting a poor tenant-screening process

Charging below market rent

Taking cash payments and relaying to you that the unit is vacant

Poor communication

High mark-ups on maintenance and repairs

Charging additional fees

Not conducting regular property inspections

Poor reporting, which can affect your taxes

In addition, the following questions are good to ask when you are interviewing a potential property manager or a property management company:

Is property management their full-time occupation? If the answer is no, you'll want to know how much time they spend on managing properties, how many properties they manage, and what systems they have in place to solve problems at your properties.

What education, experience, and credentials do they have? In my area, one of the local landlord associations provides education. Some areas require levels of certification, so you'll want to research what they are. Experience might be length of time in the business or working for other property management companies.

Have they invested time and money to become a great property manager?

Do they have insurance, staff, and a physical office? Do they have any special skills or trades that would be useful as a property manager? Do they have a vehicle that could be useful as a property manager (like a plow truck)? Do they use property management software, like Yardi? What kind of statements will they be sending you? Do they use an accounting system, like QuickBooks? How are they going to share financial information about your property with you?

Did you do a full screening of the property manager as you would a tenant?

Ask how many clients they have. Ask for references, for proof of a company, and for proof of insurance. Are they open to a criminal background check and a credit check? Are they bonded?

Do they have a written process to manage your properties with plans for when things go wrong?

Ask how they submit a request for a repair or resolution if a tenant has a problem.

See what their process is when a tenant wants to move out and for when a tenant moves in. What is the process for getting a unit ready for the next tenant after the prior tenant moves out? What do they generally do to get an apartment ready for a tenant? What kind of inspections do they do on a regular basis?

If this seems like a one-way street, remember that you can and will get fired. Yes, good property management companies will not want to deal with you. Here are the primary reasons:

Setting unrealistic expectations for rental rates.

Setting unrealistic timelines for getting or screening great tenants.

An unwillingness to spend money on upgrades to make the unit desirable to be rented to great tenants.

Not following the advice of the property manager you hired when a difficult situation occurred.

Getting emotional when something goes wrong, which often leads to a slower, more expensive situation, and then blaming the property manager for it. This can be a tenant who wants to get out of their lease early due to a financial or life-changing circumstance; a system failure, such as a fridge breaking and spoiling the tenant's food; or a mechanical failure, like a furnace breaking.

For this reason, you should always aim to be the kind of client a good property management company wants to work with. We have a great property management company for several of our units, and I am grateful for them every day. What makes them great is that we set parameters. This way they don't call me for every little problem. When there's a broken toilet or leaky faucet, they arrange the plumber and, at the end of the month, send the invoice. When we have a vacancy, they schedule the painters and contractors required to get the unit ready for the new tenants. In the unlikely event of an eviction, they handle all the paperwork required.

To quote Tony LeBlanc, a leader in property management and founder of Doorpreneur, "I'm proud to say that we turn down as much business as we take on. Not to say that these properties or clients are no good, they're just not the right fit for us. For the way that we do business."

TWO

DON'T BE A JERK

THIS PAST SUMMER, *my* WIFE AND I WERE invited to a barbecue in our neighbourhood. I was speaking to a Dalhousie University law professor about one of his lessons with new law students. He said he always begins with a chat about not being a jerk.

He explained it like this: When you're up against other lawyers in a dispute, it's better to allow exceptions, negotiate a mutually agreeable solution, and aim to be a decent person. The same is true in real estate, though unfortunately many people easily forget this. I've had many landlords contact me about how unfair a tenant or tenancy board is being. (A residential tenancy board is the governing body that generally has a province-wide jurisdiction to write a playbook with rules for both tenants and landlords to follow when it comes to renting residential properties. When there's an issue, these boards conduct a dispute-resolution process.) Some landlords have forced tenants to stay in units they can't afford after a breakup or job loss, and they become angry when a tenant moves out without notification.

I've also had landlords set unrealistic expectations for tenants when it comes to move-out cleanliness or timelines. I mean, is it realistic for a tenant to move out, clean, and get a new tenant moved in all in a single day? I've even had folks contact me bent out of shape because a buyer has asked for a one- or two-day extension on closing or conditions.

To avoid problems, here's what I recommend:

Build a reputation as a person or company that does what you say you're going to do.

Pay contractors on time. (If you need to arrange terms, talk it out, then follow through.)

Pay your bills on time. This includes property tax.

Be easy to get along with when it comes to property management. Don't question every decision they make, and trust what they have to say. Even if you don't 100% agree (like they bought a new fridge instead of searching for a used), support their decision. You hired them to make decisions so you don't have to.

I'm lucky to have had a relationship with a property management company for over a decade. Even though they manage a portfolio in a different town, I rely on their guidance, and when something breaks and they call, I just say go ahead and do it.

We've also built our relationship to a point where they don't need to call me for everything. If it's under $1,000, they know they have my approval without having to ask. It's better to not complain and whine about the cost of every single repair. Maintenance and repairs suck, but at the end of the year when you're doing your taxes, you will appreciate the expenses.

In the grand scheme of things, it doesn't matter all that much. Be reasonably flexible and easy to get along with, and it'll benefit you in the long run.

THREE

RELATIONSHIP COUNSELLING

I WAS WORKING *on* A DEMOLITION PROJECT ON A hot Sunday in July. I had to remove a few decks and decrepit outbuildings to make way for a new driveway and proper backyard on a property. I was playing beat the clock on a gravel and soil delivery, so the job had to be done as quickly as possible.

That day around noon, my wife, my business partner, and his wife with kids in tow dropped by to see if I could go boating. I told them I was in a race against time and would need to take a pass. They didn't offer to help and left quickly for the water while I slaved away on their behalf. If I could go back in time, I would have communicated my feelings and asked for their assistance. I'm sure it would have led to a productive conversation and maybe even a compromise that would've allowed us to get the demolition work done as soon as possible and still left time for time on the water.

The loneliness I felt that day was unbelievable. I ended up having a good talk with my wife and our business partner, and they agreed they should have jumped in to help complete the project. The good news is this incident opened a larger conversation that led to many changes, including my wife managing a few units herself and working in the business as more of a partner than an observer.

If you're in a relationship, I want to give you a little advice—and this doesn't just apply to real estate investing. You both need to know what you want out of the relationship and the business, and the risk tolerance and sacrifices you're each willing to make to get what you want. This may change over time, but to have a successful relationship, you need to change together.

The following are some questions you should ask each other:

- Do you want or have any desire to explore the idea of real estate investing?

- What if you break up?

- Do you like people?

- Why should we invest in real estate?

- What real estate investing strategy should we use, and how does it fit with our lifestyle?

- Who is going to manage the properties we purchase? Who will be the primary contact when problems arise with tenant relations or maintenance issues?

- What if we lose all our savings, our kids' savings, and have to start over in debt, living in a box under a bridge?

- Are you ok with tenants living in the same house as you?

- Are you comfortable being in debt for significant amounts of money, which could include home equity lines of credit, credit cards, loans from family, loans from hard-money lenders, etc.?

- If you disagree on a financial decision, who's going to mediate for you?

- Would you like to invest in an active or a passive way (active being full ownership and management, and passive being buying stocks or loaning money as your portion of the investment)?

- How much money do you have to get started?

- Do you consider being a real estate investor risky?

- If you have children and full-time jobs, how are you going to balance your time?

- Who will be the primary caregiver to the children?

If you're out of alignment with your partner on real estate investing, I recommend having an honest conversation about your life goals and aspirations. You have no idea all the ways being a landlord could affect your relationship. However, with care, attention, and focus, it can make your relationship even stronger.

FOUR

FINANCIAL LITERACY

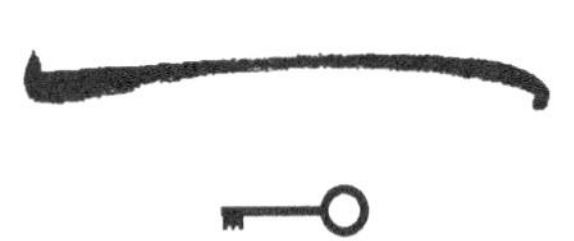

WHEN I THINK *back*, I CAN TRACE MY first step to becoming financially literate to my teenage years. Like many kids in this age range, I desired things that cost money. I figured out the only way I would get all the things I wanted was to earn money. When I was around 12 years old, I started mowing lawns. I saved most of the money I earned with the hope that one day I'd be able to purchase stuff like surfboards, skateboard components, BMX parts, and clothes.

For me, saving does not come naturally. Growing up, my father would share ideas on how to budget my money, but of course I didn't listen. It was a real struggle until eventually I left home and started to fend for myself. I had no choice but to stick to a budget or starve.

In my early 20s, it all started to click. Luckily, I never took on debt I couldn't manage and made sure to never tarnish my credit. That philosophy has paid off even to this day. Unfortunately, not everyone gets off to a good start the way I did. Knowing how to manage your own finances and having good credit are critical steps before you start investing in real estate. Otherwise, your financial house of cards could quickly crumble.

Here are a few questions you'll want to ask yourself before you make the leap into real estate:

- Do you spend more than you earn?

- Do you know how much you consistently earn?

- Have you been able to save or invest?

- Is your income protected by insurance should you find yourself too sick or injured to work?

- Do you owe any money?

- Do you know what a budget is and how it can help keep you on track?

Now let's dig into a few key components that will determine how much you can borrow, and at what rates. While good credit will certainly help, it isn't the final determining factor. The fundamentals of a credit rating come down to your ability to pay your bills, not maxing out available credit, and having open credit facilities over an extended period.

Many factors go into making up your credit score. Here are a few things you can do to know your credit score and improve it:

- Get a credit report. Websites like Credit Karma as well as most banks will provide you with a monthly update.

- Keep older credit lines open. If you must close out any credit facilities, it's better to close out newer ones as opposed to older ones.[1]

⦿ Make sure to pay your bills. I have seen many credit scores harmed by cell phone, cable, internet, power, and water bills. Many of these companies report late payments, and this can negatively affect your credit score.

The key is to have all your bills current. When you have real estate projects on the go, you will often find yourself maxing out all your available credit until the project is done. Later on you'll refinance and pay back your debts. If you have credit cards and are unable to pay the entire balance each month, make sure not to max them out. Even if that means increasing the limit, maxing out will put downward pressure on your credit rating.

Credit lines are great. I would recommend getting unsecured credit lines. That way if you can't pay off your credit card, you can transfer money from the credit line (which will likely be a much lower rate).

How do you get a line of credit? Just ask any financial institution. I would start with the larger banks, as the rates will generally be lower. Then if you need to, you can go to companies such as Easy Financial, Money Mart, or other financial institutions that are more open to lending money to people with low credit scores. Credit unions can also be a great source for getting a line of credit. Most don't have a monthly fee and only charge interest when you're carrying a balance. We have often received an unsecured credit line at the same time as a mortgage. Credit unions will often give you a credit line to pay for things like renovations and furniture. Never forget that lending institutions want to lend you money.

When you work on real estate projects, it can at times be difficult to avoid maxing out lines of credit. If that comes up, I recommend doing the best you can to limit the number of times this happens.

If you're refinancing, your lender will often add a stipulation that all or most of your current debt sources are paid off upon closing the deal. If you go with a secured credit line (like a home equity line of credit, or HELOC), you'll likely get a rate break of 3% or more.

The three main credit agencies in Canada and the U.S. are Equifax, TransUnion, and Experian. Some financial institutions will only use one of the three when they check credit.

The bottom line on credit is pay your bills and don't max out all your available credit. If you run into trouble, think long and hard about your options. I'm often shocked to find out how many people will go bankrupt over relatively small amounts of money in the $20K to $30K range. This will reflect worse than a large bankruptcy due to something like a business failure or major, one-time life event. If you can prevent it, don't let a divorce or a breakup take down your credit.

Also, watch out when it comes to consumer proposals. These can be looked at as worse than a bankruptcy. A consumer proposal is a legally binding agreement between you and your creditors (the folks you owe money to) to pay a portion of what you owe over a defined time. You will be required to pay a licensed insolvency trustee to set it up. The advantage to this method of debt repayment is that you can set up a consolidated loan and pay off your debts at a reduced rate in a defined period, such as four to five years. You will be able to keep your assets, and it protects you from collection companies as well as legal action from companies or people you owe money to. The downside of course is that it will be very difficult to borrow money while you are paying back current creditors at a reduced rate. It will have a negative impact on your credit rating equivalent to not paying your debts at all.

As your revenue increases, so will your spending. Basically, every tenant is like a little micro business giving you money that you'll need to manage. When I started out, the worst form of payment I received was cash. The problem was once I had the cash, I found it very hard to hang onto. I'm not sure the digital age is any better, especially with how easy it is to make purchases with a bank card, credit card, or phone. You'll need to monitor your spending habits on a regular basis and educate yourself on what managing money is all about to succeed on your real estate investing journey.

Wondering how you can turn things around? For the next 30 days, I want you to write down every dollar you spend. I would suggest using an app such as Mint (or your bank may have a spend-tracking function on their app). At the end of the 30 days, you will likely see areas you can reduce spending.

Budgets can be a good idea too, though I have read a lot of mixed reviews. Nevertheless, they have always served me well. In fact, when I have fallen offtrack with my spending over the years, I've reverted to writing down everything I spend and making a strict plan. I've even tried going to the bank every week and getting cash. As a real estate investor, you will need to set up a fund for repairs and maintenance, otherwise your budget will be offtrack on a regular basis due to "unexpected" expenses.

Keep in mind that budgets don't automatically mean sacrifice. For example, don't do things you hate that take time away from things that will make you money or provide enjoyment. For years I've hired someone to mow my lawn and handle my snow removal. When I first started out in real estate investing, I had a job where I was off on Fridays. That was lawn-mowing day. When I think back—what a waste of productive time. If you don't like cleaning your house, put a housecleaning service in the budget.

Spending habits can also hold you back or propel you ahead. As your income increases, you will need to keep a close eye on this. I like to refer to overspending as "leakage." You see, when you have very little money to spend and are on a tight budget, it's much easier to track your spending.

For instance, you might have a dining out budget that allows you to splurge once per week. The challenge is, when your income increases, you can easily lose track of your spending, and this can add up quickly if you love to shop or dine out.

The idea of living within your means is a financial trap that will keep you broke. I've read a lot about the concept of living within your means. I often consider this a choice because it is subjective. If I'd lived within my means for the past 20 years, I would probably be stuck financially.

Sometimes, though, you must spend money to make money. I don't want to confuse this with spending recklessly or going wildly into debt by buying a Ferrari. I'm talking about planning to improve upon your current circumstances.

My plan, and likely yours, too, since you're reading this book, is real estate. Real estate investing offers incredible choices. You can buy one six-unit property, live in one unit, and let the others pay all your bills. A great resource and starting point before you start investing in real estate is to read *Rich Dad, Poor Dad* by Robert Kiyosaki. This is an extremely popular book that will open your mind to many ideas and motivate you to get started.

FIVE

FIND A LOCAL REAL ESTATE INVESTMENT GROUP

I CAN'T REMEMBER WHAT MONTH *it* WAS, BUT THE year was 2008. My neighbour asked if I would like to join him at a local bar. He knew my wife and I were interested in getting into buy and hold real estate investing. He and his wife were also interested. In fact, he'd already done tons of research and had completed a number of property calculation spreadsheets. He told me how he found a group on a site called Meetup.com. (I recommend you check it out right now.)

The person heading up the group was a guy who was also interested in getting into rental properties (Richard Killan-Payne). I attended the meeting having no idea the journey I was about to embark on. That first small meeting determined the course my real estate investing life would take from that day forward.

Our original group soon swelled, outgrowing our meeting space. Before long, we added guest speakers. We hosted mortgage brokers, insurance brokers, private money lenders, property managers, investors with large portfolios, home inspectors, lawyers, accountants, HVAC specialists, and more. I found it incredibly helpful to be surrounded by like-minded people. When you try to talk to the masses, you will likely be faced with a ton of negativity.

It may even come from close family members. You'll hear stories of how Uncle George had rental properties and the tenants ruined his life or trashed his apartment. You will hear lots of opinions on why other investments are better than real estate, and why it isn't worth the hassle. Everyone has an opinion, and there are endless stories about bad experiences. But the same can be said for good experiences. Don't let others' fears drag you down.

As I sit and write in my dream house that has its mortgage and bills covered by rental revenue, I question why anyone would not invest in real estate. The people I have met in this real estate group have transformed my life and my family's. They have given me the confidence I needed and presented deals that I, fortunately, have been able to act upon. The networking you'll receive in these groups will help propel your investing objectives.

One major bonus is that you will quickly encounter people who are trusted industry professionals, which will save you time and money. It will also allow you to form long-lasting relationships with contractors, various tradespeople, and other investors. Since real estate investing is so broad, and it means something different to so many people, you'll get to watch and learn about many different types of investment strategies. It's also a great place to springboard ideas.

So, where can you find a local real estate group?

My two main sources at the time of writing this book are Meetup.com and Facebook. There are other places like the local classified sites like

Kijiji or Craigslist that you can utilize too. The point is, if you seek out networking opportunities, they can be used to your advantage.

Word of mouth can be another good way to hear about groups. Ask a real estate lawyer if they know of any local real estate groups, mortgage brokers, or real estate agents. And of course, there's always Google.

I feel so lucky that I was invited to that very first meeting more than a decade ago, and I can't wait to see what the future brings for myself and many other local investors.

SIX

MORTGAGES

THIS PART OF THE STORY TAKES PLACE AROUND 2011. I was attending a real estate meeting one night, and a young guy who was in his mid-to-late 20s asked me for advice on creating financial freedom through real estate. You see, he'd been able to purchase an old house with five units from a family friend. He was living in one unit at a time, fixing it up, then moving to the next. The property was located in a university district and was quite valuable.

"Should I pay off my mortgage or refinance and buy more properties?" he asked.

"It depends on what you want to do," I said. "What's your big picture objective?"

The property was already cash flow positive, and the profits were all being reinvested into the building.

"I want to set myself up to live life on my terms," he said. "I don't really want to buy more, but I've heard it's a bad idea to pay off the mortgage on a rental property because you lose the interest deduction when it's paid off."

I'd heard the same thing a time or two.

"You have to do what's right by you," I said. "You have a gift in your hand. This one property paid off will probably set you up for an uncomplicated life of financial freedom."

You see, he was reading and buying into the hype. Spending so much time around small landlords, I know people are often talked into complicated scenarios that bring in more headaches than they do cash.

Sometimes slow and steady can win the race.

Think about it this way. Is having all your mortgages paid off a good thing? Well, let's face it—on some level that is the end goal. With your own home, you may want to pay down and get a HELOC (home equity line of credit). You may also want to have a rental component to your home.

There are several tax benefits to having a rental, and you can use the rental component to pay down on your mortgage. This will allow you to build up equity that you can use to make down payments on other properties. In fact, this is what my wife and I have done with our personal home. We originally rented four suites and now just rent two.

The two suites pay for the mortgage. We can also expense things against the portion of the house that we rent. We do declare the income, so it does increase our annual income, but much of it is offset by the expenses. By doing this we get the best of both worlds. We live in a really nice large home, we get tax benefits, the rent pays our mortgage, and our equity is increasing for free. This is the power of real estate.

The tax rules in your area may help determine the best strategy for paying your mortgage. I think the main factor is personal preference and comfort. There's no right or wrong way, and every theory is opinion based, so it can be debated.

When it comes to rates, once again comfort and opinion will determine what you do. When rates are crazy low and the economy is unstable, it is unlikely rates will shoot up anytime soon. If you want a sneak peek, keep an eye on bond rates. This could be a whole other book, but here are some points on the basics based on an article from True North Mortgage about how fixed rates are determined.

According to the article, "many people don't realize the strong correlation between fixed mortgage rates and Bank of Canada bond yields."[2] Mortgages are considered riskier assets for banks than government bonds that are 100% guaranteed. Not all mortgages are paid back, so banks compensate for the higher risk with higher rates. Banks use the five-year bond yield market to determine their fixed-rate mortgage rates. In a normal market the average markup of a fixed-rate mortgage would be 1% to 2% above a secured government bond rate.[3]

According to the article, "during times of financial uncertainty, this spread can widen during 2020, as the Canadian markets were tossed around by the COVID-19 pandemic, some mortgages rates were briefly raised even though bond yields fell."[4] One final, important note—"variable rates aren't as affected, as they're tied to the prime rate."[5] Both rates can change daily, but each carries different risks—at relatively opposite ends. Generally variable rates will pay off and allow you a lower payment, more cash flow, and worst-case scenario, if rates increase, you can always lock in. When it comes to paying a mortgage off, some folks will put large down payments on properties and do short mortgage terms so they can be paid off early.

Don't worry about going against the grain of the many folks who will tell you to put the minimum down and take the longest term. The reverse of that theory is that by paying off your mortgage quickly, it can free up equity that can be converted into a secured line of credit that can be deployed anytime to purchase more properties. Do what is right for you, and you'll be fine.

Some points you'll want to consider when determining what might be right for you include the following:

- What's your risk tolerance when it comes to debt?

- Does owing money keep you up at night?

- What's your understanding of financial markets?

- What is your investing strategy? Are you trying to raise as much capital as possible for your next down payment?

- Would you rather own one property with high cash flow or several properties with lower cash flow?

SEVEN

NEGOTIATE

ONE OF *my* FIRST BUY AND HOLD REAL estate deals way back in 2009 came down to $2,000 on the price, and that is when I locked horns with the seller.

I lost out on that deal—good or bad, I'm not sure. Looking back, it seems ridiculous for $2,000 to have been a source of conflict. Why would it have made a difference if the property was worth it?

Perhaps it was my ego that got in the way of business that day. In most cases, letting emotion into a business deal is a hindrance.

Now you know what *not* to do. But what *should* you do?

What do you think of when you hear the word "negotiate"? Most of us think about the price of something. But it can, and should be, much more than that. In her best-selling real estate book, *More Than Cash Flow*, Julie Broad summed this up well, saying, "Always remember that a good negotiator is a good problem solver. A good problem solver can only be good if they actually know what problems they are trying to solve."[6] Let's make a deal!

When I started out on my real estate journey, I was into flipping houses, so I focused on things that related to my needs and rarely considered the needs of my seller. I wanted the lowest price, with the quickest closing. I often allowed my ego to drive the direction of the negotiation.

It took me a long time and cost me a lot of deals before I saw the light. I had backward, selfish thinking. Once I changed my approach, deals seemed to start happening with ease. What changed? Well, I realized that a negotiation was about way more than price. It's about learning the needs of the seller and working together on a plan that makes the deal good for everyone.

Now I enter every negotiation thinking about how I can make it a win-win for everyone.

While this type of thinking might cost me a bit of money initially, it's also important to consider the long-term cost. Here's my advice for negotiations after the due diligence process is finished.

- ⊙ Leave your emotions out of it. (This can be easier said than done.)

- ⊙ Get insight to why the seller might be selling. This information can be difficult to find out. Some people are better at uncovering these secrets than others.

My wife, Shelly, for example, can get a person's life story out of them without even trying. It's as if people just want to tell her their deepest secrets. In fact, once a tenant reached out to me and asked if they could meet with Shelly specifically to discuss a problem in their life that would force them to stop renting from us after 10 years. They could've just given notice, but they wanted to share a story with Shelly first, because they felt they couldn't leave without giving her an explanation after they'd been such a fantastic tenant for all those years.

I often feel like nobody will tell me anything. This may be partly due to the serious persona I project during business. Once I bought a property for a great price after learning the seller died. He left the property to his son, who lived in a different country and had been dealing with bad tenants in the house. I offered three important items in the negotiation of the property:

- ⊙ Cash deal

- ⊙ No conditions

- ⊙ Quick close

As a seller, I often negotiate to make my life a little easier. My wife and I were living in a two-unit property that we wanted to sell. We negotiated to rent back one of the units from the buyer after closing to give us time to find another place. We've also worked to solve problems for sellers with properties as big as a bed-and-breakfast. We knew the owners were leaving the area and would have to go through the hassle of liquidating a lot of stuff. We agreed to a higher price with the condition of them leaving it furnished (making exceptions for them to take what they wanted based on a list). This solved a problem for them and us, as we were concerned about how we were going to furnish the place.

Hard-to-sell properties can have instant solutions built in for the buyer, such as seller financing. This can also mean a better price for a cash deal. Lenders hate vacant properties, so if you're a buyer with cash, you have the upper hand. We were able to purchase one property of ours for a lower price when we discovered the seller owed back taxes and had late mortgage payments. They were likely going to lose the house anyway at some point, so we came up with a plan that allowed the seller to pay their back taxes and the mortgage. This made for a clean break on a distressed property.

I used to think negotiation was about "winning." The approach when I first started out was "How can I take it all and feel as if I have won?" What I've discovered on my real estate journey is that when I focus on a win-win negotiation style, the deals work out better for everyone.

REAL ESTATE AGENTS

I N THE SPRING OF 2009, WE *had* OUR buy and hold company ready to go. Armed with down payment money that was burning a hole in our pocket, we connected with a real estate agent we knew. We shared our plan and went to work. I'm not sure how many properties we looked at, but let's just say lots.

A great real estate agent can make you wealthy. They can get you access inside many properties and show you these properties before they hit the market. Here's what you should look for in a real estate agent:

- ⊙ Someone who can find you deals

- ⊙ Someone who takes the time to figure you out as a person (what type of deals you want, your "why," and your investment goals)

- ⊙ Someone who is patient

- ⊙ Someone who isn't easily offended

- ⊙ Someone who doesn't let emotion or ego get in the way of a negotiation

- ⊙ Someone who understands that you may look at several properties and only offer on a few

- ⊙ Someone who understands that investment property closing timelines are often much longer than regular residential closings

- ⊙ Someone who can bring you deals and suggest solutions on how you could make it happen

- ⊙ Someone who is an amazing negotiator and problem solver

- ⊙ Someone who thinks like a detective and figures out why the seller is selling and can use this info to help with the negotiation process

- ⊙ Someone who isn't afraid to make phone calls

- ⊙ Someone who understands vendor take backs and seller financing

- ⊙ Someone who is connected to people and can offer various lending solutions

Don't feel bad for working with several different real estate agents at once either. Let agents know up front that you are happy to deal with them but that you're looking for folks who can bring you deals that meet your criteria. If you're finding the deals yourself, then contacting the same agent to get you in for a viewing, who is working for who?

You may also encounter opportunities for cash sales, private-sale deals, and more. In my early days, I was nervous about cash deals that involved lawyers. That changed one day when I did my first private-sale deal. Our lawyer walked me through the process, drew up a purchase and sale agreement, and dealt mostly lawyer to lawyer to get the deal done.

Then one day I was selling an old wreck of a house on a great piece of land. I put an ad on a local classified site, met a buyer, and showed him the property. We went to a local coffee shop to hash out a deal. All I had for a contract was a lined notepad.

We sketched out a purchase and sale agreement, signed a copy each, shook hands, and handed it to our respective lawyers. As the buyer, he had his lawyer craft it into a more legible and proper purchase and sale agreement. Then he sent it to my lawyer so I could review it. A few weeks later, we closed, and I had money in the bank with very little expense.

When you're a real estate investor, you need a down-to-earth, deal-savvy agent with common sense and nerves of steel. My all-time greatest real estate purchase may never have happened if it were not for my friend and agent Nick Harvey who gave me the confidence to move forward after sharing his past experiences renting to students.

Are our deals complex? The truth is, compared to a buy and sell agreement with a nuclear family where both parents have steady jobs, minimal criteria, good credit, and only one home, yes, I suppose real estate investing is complex.

In my experience, here are a few of the things that make deals as an investor more complex than a more traditional home-buying experience:

- ⊙ *No emotion*: Real estate investors don't tend to fall in love with a property. It's more about the cash flow or potential appreciation. If a bidding war ensues, or the numbers don't work once the expenses are verified, an investor will quickly walk away.

This can be annoying to an agent who's not used to working with investors.

⊙ *Down payments*: The government requires you to use unencumbered down payment money to purchase an income property. You can use secured line of credit money, but not unsecured line of credit money. You can't use credit cards. The lender will often ask for bank records and proof of the source of income to ensure they've done everything possible to follow the rules.

⊙ *Non-owner-occupied rules*: Currently lenders in Canada require a 20% down payment on properties that are not going to be owner occupied. If it's an owner-occupied property, they only require 5% down.[7] You may be asked to provide proof that you intend to live in the property you are buying.

⊙ *Multiple partners:* When one property has multiple partners or buyers.

⊙ *Vendor take backs*: This involves asking for vendor take backs on deals, and the seller finances part of the transaction, usually in the form of a second mortgage.

⊙ *Commercial component to the deal*: Lenders have separate criteria for commercial properties. They fit in a different category, and this can be good or bad. However, with an inexperienced agent and buyer, they may offer on a building that could have a commercial and residential component. The commercial component in Canada will be subject to local tax (in my area it's 15%). It may also be tougher to get financed.

⊙ *Condition length can be longer than a regular single-family transaction*: Many new investors who work with inexperienced agents will set a 10-day condition expectation. That will likely not work. When you own more than one property, the lender will want to know about the financial status of all your properties. This often requires additional paperwork, such as copies of signed lease agreements. They may ask for proof of the legal use of the property. They may also want a physical appraisal.

- *Area the purchase is in*: Your lender might hold up a deal based on an area. Some lenders will not lend at all or may lend less money for a property depending on the area where it is located. We see this a lot lately where the real estate market is overvalued versus assessments. This makes investors look at secondary markets (outside of main areas). A lender may not want to lend you money for a property in a known rough area or a rural area because they consider it too risky. This may force an investor to walk away, renegotiate the deal, put more money down, or find a different lender.

- *Financial information to provide your lender and lawyer*: If you plan on investing in real estate, it's a good idea to build a small portfolio of relevant documents to make transactions easier. This list will include, but is not limited to,

    - Income verification

    - Letter of employment

    - Voided cheque

    - Current copies of existing leases on rental properties you own

    - Two pieces of signed picture ID, such as a driver's licence and passport

    - Expense information from the property you're buying (electric and utility bills)

Also keep on hand a number for a home inspector, lawyer, and any other inspectors you plan to use on a regular basis.

To think about it now, I realize that some investors are high maintenance. So, why would an agent want to deal with them? The answer is simple. Volume. A regular buyer may only buy one or two houses in a lifetime. However, an investor will be buying several. This makes learning how to deal with real estate investors a worthwhile endeavour for many agents. It all comes down to communication. Do not be afraid to express your objectives and criteria when you meet with real estate agents. Your business depends on it.

LENDERS, MORTGAGE BROKERS, AND BANKS

MY WIFE AND I *were* SITTING IN A familiar office at a major bank. We had an appointment that day to meet with a mortgage broker who represented this bank. The bank had loaned us hundreds of thousands of dollars for many projects over the previous seven years. We were hanging out, feeling quite confident about what the outcome of the forthcoming meeting was going to be.

The only difference this time was that we were getting into buy and hold real estate investing and wanted to buy the properties under a company name. All our previous properties were straightforward and purchased in our personal name.

At the time, we had our newborn baby sleeping in his carrier. We presented the idea of buying some rental properties with a friend of ours and putting them in a company name. The gentleman looked at us as if we were presenting some sort of crazy idea, even though we were all employed professionals with money for a down payment.

He said he would check with a secondary lending division of this major bank. A couple of days later, he called to let us know it would not be possible. We were somewhat shocked. If a major bank wouldn't lend to us, we would be screwed. I started asking around about alternative lenders and sought advice from other people who owned rental properties and had them financed.

My challenge was that I'd dealt with this particular bank my entire life. I felt loyal to them, even though they could not give me what I wanted. This all changed when I met my current mortgage broker. We arranged a meeting, and this time it was me, my wife, and my business partner. We asked him what we needed to do to buy a two-unit property in a company name.

"Do you have the money for a down payment?"

"Yes, we do," I said.

"Perfect. Go find a property," he said.

My jaw dropped. Could it really be that easy? I told him how we were turned down by the bank. He explained how bank mortgage reps are restricted to providing their products, so they don't always have the product you need. He said that we would all be co-signing the loans, so even though the properties would all be in the corporation's name, we would be responsible for the loan defaults if the company stopped paying the loans. (Special note—in the U.S., some lenders will lend to a company for properties with a nonrecourse clause.[8] This means the company and shareholders will not be responsible if the payments stop being made. First, you'll want to pay your mortgage obligations, and second, lenders are usually only open to a nonrecourse loan if a significant down payment has been made. So it's generally in favour of the lender should you stop making payments.)

He also said we should discuss a strategic plan for what lenders we use, and when, while we build our portfolio. I took great comfort when he suggested my job was to find the deals and his job was to find the financing for them.

It turns out that banks, and for that matter all lending institutions, not only carry the majority of the power when it comes to property "ownership" but are fair-weather friends. Loyalty to a particular lender is generally unnecessary for any length of time. Yes, it's convenient to have all your mortgages and banking with one organization. But unfounded loyalty may stall your progress.

Most lenders have specialties. This can change over time, so it's important to be connected with a strong, experienced mortgage broker who knows what lenders will take what deal.

Let me give you an example. One of our deals was on a six-unit apartment building. Usually that would go to a commercial lender. At the time, our mortgage broker said he had a lender that would treat it like a residential mortgage if we put 30% down. This allowed us to get a 3% loan with a 30-year amortization and forgo a mandatory phase one environmental inspection and appraisal. It turned into a loan that was similar to financing a regular house. This simplified and sped up the whole deal.

Mortgage brokers with rental property experience are critical for other reasons as well. When you purchase rental properties, the deals can be more complicated. How the deal is presented to the lender can mean the difference between an approval or not. If you end up with a mortgage broker who isn't familiar with rental properties, they'll likely get tired of dealing with you.

I mean let's face it—we're not that easy to deal with. Our financial picture is usually complicated (multiple streams of income). We live our lives trying to expense as much as possible, which can cause problems when it comes to trying to show gross income. We often start the purchase and finance process on properties that just don't work out for various reasons.

We're always trying to stretch the rules and terms to maximize cash flow, often have other partners involved in the property, include complex add-ons like vendor take backs, and want loans written with the intent to renovate and refinance within a short period of time. Unfortunately, this makes every deal that much harder to navigate.

To make things easier, you'll want to keep the financial component of the deal as simple as possible. Here are some tips you can use:

- ⊙ Find a mortgage broker who has experience with real estate investors and lending on investment properties.

- ⊙ Have a portfolio ready with your personal financial picture. This should include but is not limited to the following:

  - Pay stubs

  - Income sources

  - Two years' notices of assessments

  - A voided cheque

  - A list of assets

  - A list of liabilities

  - A list of any credit challenges, such as bankruptcy

  - How much you have to put down

  - Explanation of any down payment sources that involve a joint venture partner or vender take back

  - Documentation of preapproval from your mortgage broker

To sum it up, get referred to a mortgage broker with rental income and financing experience who has access to multiple lenders (including private money). Don't let loyalty to a particular lender slow down or stall your progress as an investor.

Alternative Lenders

When you hear the term "alternative lender," does that sound like a fancy name for loan shark? While I don't have much experience directly with alternative lenders or lenders of private money, I know several people who are private lenders or are quite familiar with them. From what I know, here's what I can offer as advice: if the deal is good enough, you won't have trouble getting money.

Here's another little secret: Do not focus on the interest rate you are being charged by the alternative lender. Look at the profitability of the deal. Usually, alternative lenders will charge a higher rate, but other than an up-front fee, the payments are often set up as interest-only while the money is in your hands. If you feel the interest rate you're being charged on the short-term money borrowed from an alternative or hard-money lender is too high, you likely should not be doing the deal.

Here is how you can find alternative mortgage lenders:

- Ask a mortgage broker.

- Check around at your local investment group.

- Inquire at a local bank.

- Run a Google search.

You will be surprised how many are around. Here are some examples:

- ⊙ Atlantic Signature Mortgage & Loan

- ⊙ Alternative Mortgage Solutions

- ⊙ CMI Mortgage Investments

If you have a business that will make lots of cash in a short period of time and is risk-free, you will find the money. The biggest challenge is that the deal needs to cover the cost of borrowing the cash. Private money is awesome for when you find undervalued properties.

Here are typical terms you can expect when working out a deal:

- ⊙ A 65% loan to value (value based on appraisal)

- ⊙ An up-front fee of 10% or $10,000 for every $100K borrowed

- ⊙ Interest-only, monthly payments with a higher interest rate of 10% to 15%

- ⊙ A three-year term with a clause to allow you to pay out early or extend if necessary

Many are set up as vehicles that you can invest in if you don't want to deal with tenants, construction, etc. They'll often be set up as MICs (Mortgage Investment Corporation), which are an investment vehicle that can be set up with a minimum investment amount.

A much more passive way to invest is in real estate. You may also find a person with cash looking for steady, hassle-free retirement income. Mortgage brokers, lawyers, financial advisers, and real estate agents often have access to these folks. They generally only want to lend on a few properties up to a certain dollar amount. If you're the right client, it can be a great way to acquire control of properties and provide someone with an income.

Just keep in mind that with these types of deals, the borrower will usually be responsible for the broker fee, down payment, appraisal, and legal fees associated with the loan. Just be careful so you don't get in over your head.

TEN

THE IMPORTANCE OF LAWYERS

IN THE SUMMER *of* 2012, I BOUGHT A two-unit property set up as a bungalow with a basement apartment. My wife and I got a call from our lawyer's office asking for a zoning certificate because it appeared that the house was only zoned for a single-family home. Our agent contacted the seller's agent to find out if they had a zoning certificate to confirm that the unit was legal. Unfortunately, they did not.

Our lawyer's office sprang into action and did some digging. Since the unit was about 50 years old, they tried to find out if the unit had a permit when it was originally constructed. It turned out one of the past owners obtained a nonconforming certificate, making the apartment legal. I know this is not a very exciting story, but it's just one of the many instances in which a lawyer can protect you. In this case, if we didn't produce a document stating that the property was legally a two-unit property, we would have had to cancel the deal or move forward knowing there was a risk of a city inspector shutting it down.

In instances like this one, your lawyer could be your most important relationship in your real estate business. And depending on how large you plan to grow your business or what other businesses you're involved in, you may want to form a relationship with a full-service law firm. At the very least, you'll want someone who is an expert in real estate transactions and frequently deals with real estate investors.

Your lawyer should also be able to help you with handling the following items:

- Corporation and LLC setup
- Vendor take back contracts
- Joint venture contracts
- Down payments from multiple sources
- Purchase and sale agreements for private sales
- Mortgage and lending agreement document reviews
- Funding holdbacks if there are problems at closing
- Explanations of easements
  - Right of ways
  - Proper land use
  - Property use

Your legal team is often the glue and the voice of reason that may keep your deal together. A good legal team can direct a deal from start to finish. They collect important documents and find out as much as possible about the property in order to protect the buyer. Often with smaller properties, documents are hard to get or do not exist. For example, a basement suite may get added to a house without prior consultation with the local municipality. Proper zoning, legal usage, and confirmation of ownership are the key components for your legal team.

If you're planning to change the usage of the property or redevelop it, you need someone with experience in local zoning rules. These can be very complex. Your legal team is generally the middle person in the deal and will collect all information on your behalf, including tax information, utility bills, zoning letters, building permits, and mortgage information. All the changes will be reviewed by your legal team. When the deal is done and money changes hands, they arrange it. If the deal falls apart and deposits need to be returned, they handle that as well.

In fact, I will let you in on a secret. Your legal team can handle the whole transaction, and you often don't even need a real estate agent. Don't be afraid to go after off-market properties or find private-sale deals. I wish I knew this earlier, but the real estate agents I always worked with gave me the impression that an agent always *had* to be involved.

On this topic, I will offer a few words of caution. Many lenders will want details on the property that are found on MLS (Multiple Listing Service) cut sheets—room dimensions, tax information, and things like zoning documents—so be prepared to provide this information or to pay somebody to build a cut sheet for you.

The easiest way to get an MLS cut sheet is to use an existing one from a previous sale (you will need to verify accuracy) or work out a deal with a licensed realtor or for sale by owner company. It's easy to find what information is required with a quick Google search. Realtor and Viewpoint are two websites that can help you find what you need.

When I started out, I asked around for the cheapest legal team. But I've learned since then that cheaper is not always better—and in the long run, the perceived cheapest option may even end up being more expensive.

As I've learned and experienced more in my life and business, my wife and I use a law firm for all things legal. It's not necessarily cheap, but our firm is a good one and gets things done efficiently.

Here are a few reasons you might need a full-service law firm:

- ◉ Real estate related

  - Small-claims court disputes

  - Boundary- and property-line disputes

  - Corporation and LLC setup

  - Contract document creation (purchase and sale, joint venture, vendor take backs)

  - Title searches and owner verification

  - Release and proof of mortgages that are paid out

  - Lien disputes (contractors often put liens on buildings)

  - Clarification of capital gains and and how to tax-efficiently sell a property

  - Share or asset purchase due diligence and advice for the best way to handle a purchase or sale

  - Assistance with lawsuits

- ◉ Non–real estate related

  - Creation of LLCs or corporations for other business ventures

  - Wills

  - Copyright disputes

  - Trademark creation

  - Witnesses for notarizing documents

  - Divorce

As I travel on my journey through life and business, I take comfort in the fact that I have a great lawyer I can call upon at any time with legal questions. I consider my lawyer (who is now a partner in the law firm we deal with) a true friend.

ELEVEN

ACCOUNTING

IN THE BEGINNING *many* YEARS AGO, WE HAD a book-keeper who did our annual taxes. She mostly did personal taxes and bookkeeping for individuals but also worked for a few local restaurants as a side hustle in addition to her full-time accounting job. When we decided to get into buy and hold investing, we just assumed she would take it on. She did for the first few properties; however, it became clear that we would require additional help and expertise, so she basically fired us and told us we'd need to find a replacement.

This was completely understandable, because at times I feel bad for the number of questions I need to ask of these folks. This is part of the reason I'm so grateful they are available to help me work through issues as they come up.

Let's start by thinking about a riddle. There were three accountants sitting at a bar. A guy walks up and asks all three the same question. Each one provides a different answer. How do you know which one is right? The reality is they may be all right, or at least partially right. Many accounting questions are answered with an opinion-based answer.

I may not know all the answers; however, I am going to strongly recommend you find good people to help you with this end of your business. The bean counting is incredibly important, and it's critical you know what they can do for you and what limitations they may have.

If you expect a bookkeeper to know all about tax law and what can and cannot be expensed, you will be set up for disappointment. The lines all too often get blurred between a bookkeeper, general accountant, and a tax accountant by people who don't know better. I mean they all deal with numbers, right?

As your business grows, so too will your needs. At first, you might only need some light bookkeeping and somebody to do your tax return. But as things get more complicated, you may need other specialists to lend a helping hand in order to keep your books straight.

Now let's take a deeper look at who does what.

The Bookkeeper

This is who keeps track of money coming in and money going out. They will often be familiar with programs like QuickBooks and will likely print your basic financial statements each year upon request.

Since it's a clerical role, bookkeeping is generally quite inexpensive from a billable-hours perspective. Not often would a bookkeeper provide or be qualified to talk about business strategy. To save money, I recommend keeping your receipts neat and organized. Also note any changes to tenants or rent.

We've all seen a business owner who gives bags or shoe boxes of receipts to their accountant in the movies. Well, in real life accountants hate it just as much as they do in the movies. I was consulting not long ago with a couple who had just inherited a small portfolio of properties. Some of the tenants were not paying rent, so step one was to locate the leases. The unfortunate part was the entire filing system for the properties was a couple of laundry baskets filled with papers.

Some property management companies will keep bookkeeping records for what they do for your properties, so a lot of the work will be done. I provide invoices to our bookkeeper every six months.

Our bookkeeper does not prepare our tax returns. For that we have a tax accountant. He specializes in tax returns and knows how to save us money on taxes. Whoever you have doing your tax returns, make sure they are familiar with tax rules around rental properties because, as you may or may not know, a big benefit to owning real estate is the tax benefits.

Accountant

The term "accountant" is often used very broadly and often describes anyone from a bookkeeper to someone who sets up offshore family trusts. What you need as a business owner and investor is somebody with the right expertise to handle all things financial for you. As you grow, so will your accounting needs. Eventually you'll start dealing with specific kinds of accountants, like chartered accountants (CA), certified public accountants (CPA), or certified management accountants (CMA).

Those who have designations generally charge more and may only be available in larger, full-service accounting firms. These folks may be required to provide documents to auditors (whether it's self-imposed or imposed by the IRS or CRA). They will also ensure your company is as tax efficient as possible. This may include business strategy, filling out forms for government programs and grants, setting up family trusts, or other more complex tax-saving instruments that are common in big business.

Keep in mind accounting could be a whole separate book, so I will stick with the basics for the purposes of this section. Here are a few ways accounting can benefit your business:

- ⊙ *Consultations for business setup*: When it comes to setting up corporations or LLCs, the lines get blurred between accountants and lawyers. How you set up or don't set up may have a serious impact on your finances in the future.

- ⊙ *Depreciation*: In general, buildings depreciate, and land appreciates.[9] When a building depreciates, it's an expense that will reduce your revenue but save you tax in the short term. Now, be warned, when you go to sell, this can be problematic. If you've been avoiding the tax man over the years and have depreciated your building to zero, you will likely have to pay a bigger tax bill for the property.

- ⊙ *Capital cost versus expense*: This is super important to understand, and if you don't, you'll need to have an accountant who does. A capital expenditure adds value and usable life to a property. It's the opposite of depreciation but cannot be expensed, so in the short term, it may not have a benefit to you. A simple example might be windows. If you replaced one rotten window at a time, that could be considered an expense. But if you replaced them all at once, that could be considered a capital improvement. Think of expenses as a short-term benefit and capital improvements as a long-term benefit.

Expenses: One advantage to having rental properties is that you never have a shortage of items to expense. Some things will be basic maintenance and repairs. This includes parts and labour. There will be times when you have an overtime call for a plumber, and at the time it seems bad. Then, at the end of the year, you get to expense it and reduce your income. Other items might be office supplies, bank fees, interest payments, or gas in your vehicle. (See CRA details, as they require a log.) You can expense anything that's required to earn you rental income.

The bottom line is that if you keep your expenses reasonable, you'll likely stay off the radar. If you're contacted by the CRA or IRS, it's important not to panic. Occasionally I've been asked to send some supporting documents to back up a claim. This is another great reason to keep a proper filing system.

Even if you're asked to pay tax that you do not agree with, you may want to consider paying the bill and then filing a notice of objection. You're basically saying, "Here's your money up front, but I object and intend to get it back." The advantage is that it stops the clock on additional penalties and fees. If it's for a large amount, you may want to consider a tax lawyer.

Keep in mind that the job of the tax man is to collect tax. They send letters that are designed to intimidate and shake the bushes. It is a powerful organization with huge reach and resources, so tread lightly if you have become selected for an audit. If you have blatantly broken tax laws, don't run and hide. Instead, make a deal and remember its primary focus is collecting what you owe.

In summary, make sure to get accounting help that meshes with your requirements. When you file your personal and corporate tax returns, keep all supporting documents in a safe, organized location for several years. The IRS website seems a bit clearer on the length of time required to keep documents (three years minimum)[10] compared to the CRA website (around six years).[11] The grey area is that both say that if they detect fraud or intentional tax evasion, they may ask for more supporting documents over a longer period.

To cover all our bases, here's how we are set up. When we first started our real estate journey, I figured I would do the accounting. I have an accounting background, after all. But I was quickly overwhelmed as we built our portfolio. That's when I hired two key professionals: One was a tax specialist accountant, and the other was a bookkeeper.

The tax specialist handles our year-end tax return and provides advice when it comes to the difference between a capital improvement or a repair expense. They're also tasked with finding ways to minimize our tax bill, providing advice for when we should depreciate buildings, explaining how taxable gains work, and telling us how to get money out of the company for personal use as tax efficiently as possible.

When you choose a tax accountant, make sure they're familiar with income property owners. The tax benefits around owning rental properties are one of the key reasons you'll want to be in the rental property business, so it's critical that you know all the rules in order to reap the tax-break benefits available.

Your tax accountant can also keep you updated on any new rules and make sure you do not stray offtrack. For example, here's a trouble area that's common for property owners. Let's say you're laying flooring in a rental unit, and you oversupply the project. Instead of wasting material, you tell the contractor to install the extra material in your personal home and bill it to the rental unit. This is clear fraud, but it's quite common.

Some solid advice on the flip side of this are warnings about what might be considered a capital improvement (something that enhances the value and life of a building) versus something that can be expensed to reduce the current year's tax bill. Capital improvements are a great hedge against capital gains taxes when you sell. However, in the short term, expenses can be better if you plan on holding your properties for an extended period of time.

An example is if you replace one window in a property, that would be a maintenance and repair expense. If you replaced all the windows at one time, that would be a capital improvement. To expense the job, the right option is to replace the windows one at a time.

As your business grows, or if you get to a point where you want to sell some properties, advice from a good tax accountant can save you thousands.

TWELVE

CONSTRUCTION AND INSPECTION TEAMS

I WAS ON A BUYING SPREE, WHICH REQUIRED A team. We became very close, and each member knew exactly what to look for. Together, we were like a team of ants. Once we secured a viewing or secured a property with an offer and a clause to view, we got the team together and descended on the property to check it out.

The market you're operating in will determine the potential limitations to getting the right people on-site to look at a property. The team I assembled consisted of a home inspector, plumber, electrician, sewer pipe videographer, general contractor, and depending on the location, a radon tester. I'm a big believer in due diligence and would advise you not to go the cheap route in this area. Another thing to consider is that even if you're in a fiercely competitive market and waived the inspection clause, you still have an opportunity to view the property and can back out later if the team decides it's not a wise investment.

The properties I was interested in were generally at least 60 years old, so the electrical and plumbing usually needed upgrades. The awesome part about having a team involved is you could plan and set up the renovation work prior to the closing. That allowed us to be way more efficient on our construction turnaround time.

My team was always eager to work with me since it gave them an advanced look at a job, and if I moved forward, it was guaranteed work. As a result, we bonded and had fun at most of these showings. For out-of-town properties you may need to use technology like FaceTime or Skype if you cannot attend in person.

Home Inspectors

Whether you need a home inspector or not is a topic that comes up often. In a fiercely competitive market, pressure is often put on buyers to waive the clause. This pressure can lead to an inexperienced buyer getting in over their head on the renovation or usage of a property.

When people are buying properties sight unseen for huge amounts of money, it can be irritating to lose out on a deal because your competitor didn't have the inspection clause. Depending on your comfort level and the price of the property, you will often use your experience to determine whether you wish to move forward with a property without an inspection. Some properties such as tax sales and many foreclosure sales do not permit an inspection.

An interesting story that happened not too long ago is about a company named Zillow. They were originally a lead-generation company for realtors, real estate buyers, and sellers. During the great property boom during the COVID-19 pandemic, they decided to get into the house-flipping business. Their first step was to offer their platform to house flippers free of charge in order to collect data. They used an algorithm that they figured was fail safe, and armed with investor money, they started a program so that a homeowner could generate an instant cash offer. They started buying everything based on math, and for the most part, it was done sight unseen and for a high price.

In the end, after being accused by many for price-fixing and overpaying for thousands of homes, they started to lose huge sums of money. Now they're backing off, selling these properties, and going back to the original plan of lead generation. It was a very expensive lesson that ended up hammering their stock price and bottom line.

As you acquire experience, you'll learn to look for certain things when searching for a property. Many areas will have similar homes built in certain areas, so the trend can be easy to pick out. In the Northeast of the U.S. and Canada, we have a lot of houses built as early as the mid-1800s. They tend to have characteristics in common, such as damp basements as well as roofs, sidings, and windows that are beat up by the extreme weather patterns.

The older houses were usually built without safety in mind, and the features may or may not still exist. This can include lead paint, arsenic wallpaper, lead pipes, and knob and tube wiring. Some of the things inside other homes may not be much better. There are asbestos, lead, siding, plaster, insulation, pipe wrapping, and flooring materials that will all need to be inspected. Once you know what to look for, it's easy to pick out. That being said, a lot of times it's based on an assumption according to the year the house was built. If you want to be 100% sure, you will need to have it tested at a lab.

Some common places to find asbestos would be in plaster walls, pipe insulation, vinyl floors, acoustic ceiling tiles, vermiculite insulation, and certain types of siding and roofing shingles.

And of course, I could not go through this section without mentioning

Kitec plumbing. It's estimated that 292,000 North Americans have the product in their homes.[12] It's unknown how many of those homes are in Canada, but it was widely used in the late 1990s and early 2000s before it was recalled, as both the fittings and pipes were prone to deterioration.[13] Kitec, billed as a cheaper and easy-to-install alternative to copper piping, was used primarily in hot water baseboard and in-floor heating systems. The product may also have other brand names, including PlumbBetter, IPEX AQUA, and WarmRite. It can be identified by its bright-orange (hot water) and bright-blue (cold water) covering. The piping is also la-belled with the identifier "ASTM 1281."[14]

That's not to mention many houses were either poorly insulated or lacked insulation. I can remember buying a house as late as 2010 that was built in the 1930s and getting a call from my electrician who said he had good news and bad news. He said the bad news was there wasn't a stitch of insulation in the exterior walls of the top floor. The good news was that it would make it way easier to fish wires. You see, the previous owners insulated the main floor but not the upper floor.

The point is all these things can add up, and you'll get used to seeing them, so it will limit your dependence on a home inspector. I still like to have my trusted home inspector view our properties as needed. The reason I put value in a home inspector is because they're not looking for work—they're just pointing out the facts.

If the property sucks and does not work for you, you have three choices:

1. Buy it and shut up.

2. Ask the seller for a concession on the price.

3. Don't buy it.

Pretty simple.

The limitation of the inspector comes down to the fact that they can only inspect what they can see, so don't be surprised if you must bring in a specialist like an electrician, plumber, or other specialist after the inspection to get a second opinion and get a quote for repairs. This is why it's important to have a full team with you when you go for an inspection if you can manage to swing it.

Plumber

Old houses usually need plumbing work. This will require a video of the drainage system out to the road, so a plumber with a video system or a contact with a plumbing videographer will be necessary.

Keep in mind that plumbing problems are not just in old houses. Even new construction can have issues. Getting a thorough inspection before you buy can save you a lot of money down the road when you realize you've got an expensive problem that needs to be dealt with.

Electrician

The modern demands for electricity in homes are much greater than in the past. The code has completely changed as well. We've gone from a time when one or two plugs per room on the same circuit was ok to a time when most building codes require multiple plugs per room, plus hardwired smoke detectors in every bedroom. In fact, in many instances properties (especially multifamily) need to have the entire electrical system upgraded right from the street. You need extra juice to meet the current everyday demands of heat pumps, a full complement of appliances, and more electronics than ever.

General Contractor

This person can bring it all together. Usually, these individuals are carpenters by trade or window, door, and siding specialists. The general contractor (GC) may also act as a project manager after you own the property.

If you're doing a small renovation, the GC will bring in all the tradespeople necessary to do the renovation, that way you don't have to contact everyone individually. For example, if you're doing a kitchen renovation the GC will rip out the old cabinets, order the new ones, and arrange the install. A great GC will make the overall project seem smooth and painless.

On the other hand, if you were to do it all on your own without a GC, you would need to arrange junk removal, contact a cabinet maker, arrange a plumber, and likely, hire an electrician. This could take a lot of time and coordination. A GC will arrange it all and quote the job as a complete package. If you have a specific skill set and time on your hands, you can ask to be the subcontractor. On many of my projects, I've played the role of the demolition man. I'm not very handy, but I do like to rip things apart. The general contractor is an important part of your team.

Radon Tester

There are many areas that have high concentrations of radon. This gas basically causes cancer. A simple test can determine if the property has radon. There is also a simple solution of a radon-removal fan, so it's not the end of the world should you have radon. The concentration levels in North America seem to be literally all over the map. Check out Eco-Home for more detailed information.[15]

Project Manager

Depending on the size of the project and the expertise required, you may need an official project manager. If it's a smaller project, you can do it yourself (if you have time for multiple site visits) or have a general contractor do it. The property management company that will be managing the property once the renovation is complete may also serve as a project manager.

The project manager keeps everything on track and makes sure the project gets done efficiently and on time. Project managers have helped me countless times. Once I had an extensive renovation going on where plumbers, drywall folks, electricians, and painters all had to stay in an efficient sequence. Unfortunately, many tradespeople take on multiple jobs at once, so it's not uncommon for them to not show up when they're supposed to. Of course, that sometimes causes the project to get behind.

My project manager would stay in constant communication with the owners of the trade companies we were dealing with. He noticed a trend on the first week and dropped by on a Friday morning and paid everyone for the week. He then dropped by later that afternoon around 2:30 p.m., and the site was empty. From that day forward, the new time for weekly paycheques was 4:30 p.m. on Friday afternoons. This made a difference right off the bat—not just the extra two hours of work, but also the fact that he stopped by multiple times to check on progress kept them on track. You see, the painter can't come in until the drywall is done, and the drywallers can't come in until the electricians and plumbers are done, and so on and so on.

Structural Engineer

There are times when you might need a structural engineer on a project, especially if you got a good deal on a property with structural issues.

I live in an area with full basements. Sometimes the foundations were slapped together and are full of cracks or are shifting. The good news is with the help of a structural engineer, it might be just a matter of jacking the house and putting a new foundation under it. This can lead to the possibility of at least one additional unit, maybe two.

Environmental Engineer

This is usually only for bigger projects. It often will depend on the lender's requirements. There are different levels for this type of inspection, which range from observation to extensive research on the property (what was there before) or a full-site cleanup. The latter may be needed due to previous contamination, like underground oil tanks or fuel tank removal.

If you're into small multifamily properties, typically under five units, you will likely never get asked for an assessment from an environmental engineer.

INSURANCE

ONE RAINY *sunday* MORNING IN FEBRUARY, I WAS at a coffee shop with my family when I realized I had three missed calls and a voicemail. They were all from a long-term tenant who never caused problems.

"The basement is filling up with water," she said in the voicemail. For as chill and laid-back as she sounded, we had a situation on our hands. The sewer backed up, so it wasn't just water spewing into the basement. I jumped into my car and headed right over. Approximately three inches of water covered the floors in the finished basements of my side-by-side duplex.

I called my insurance broker, and he sprang into action. Within hours I had a plumber pumping out water and a disaster renovation company cutting out the bottom four feet of the walls, removing flooring, and installing large fans to dry it out. One tenant had insurance; the other tenant did not.

Keep in mind that while insurance maybe the least sexy part of real estate investing, it can also prevent you from buying certain properties. Insurance is one of the most expensive components of having properties. In recent years the cost has gone through the roof and, in some cases, has turned cash flowing properties into cash negative properties. This can include a personal home or investment property. Prior to getting into buying investment properties, I used to just leave my insurance requirements in the hands of a broker. I trusted at face value that they knew what they were doing and were providing the right coverage.

This continued with a couple of rental properties I owned. They sent the insurance that the bank required (which is minimal). But then it all changed at a real estate investor meeting. One night, the guest speaker was a commercial insurance broker. When he began to speak about the coverages that investors should consider, I went into shock.

At the time, I didn't have sewer backup insurance, lost rental payment coverage, or many other coverage options he spoke about. After that meeting I had a friend refer me to a proper commercial insurance agent, and the rest is history. Over the next several years, I did have a sewer backup claim and a tenant who sued for a slip and fall, which were all handled smoothly because of my coverage.

When I needed it most, I was glad to be covered. I had a house fire in my personal home (which has a rental component). The claim was for hundreds of thousands, and boy, was I glad I had it insured as needed.

Now I ask many questions of my broker, and we review our policies annually. (If your broker is not doing this, I would recommend you change your broker.) I mean simple things, like the high cost of building supplies, could put you in a situation where you do not have your building insured for enough money. Also, as investors, you need to get educated on the terminology used in the business. With Intact Insurance (the company my home is insured with), these are some key coverages relating to water damage with adjustable limitations that people don't often think of until it is too late:

- ◉ *Sewer backup*: Coverage in the event water backs up from the sewer system and flows into your home. This is important coverage for your rental properties. This expands into areas such as toilets backing up and leaking down below. It does not cover ground water or rising water tables.

- ◉ *Overland water*: Coverage for water damage caused by lake or river overflow, heavy rain, or rapid snowmelt that enters your home from a point at or above the ground surface. This does not cover flooding caused by waves, storm surges, ground water, landslides, or rising water tables.

- ◉ *Ground water*: Coverage for damage caused by water entering your home suddenly and accidently through a basement wall, foundation, floor, or rising water table. This doesn't cover flooding caused by waves, storm surges, or damage caused by earth movement or landslides.

The reality is that each section or coverage has a breakdown like this. Other than reading the lengthy book of documents or becoming an insurance agent yourself, you need to find a knowledgeable insurance broker who understands your personal risk tolerance, that way you will always have the right coverage for the right price.

You also need to disclose your tenant profile to your insurance agent. I was surprised to learn recently that some insurance companies will not insure you if you rent to students. It's often right in the policy. The insurance company may also want to know how many people will be occupying each unit.

If you have a regular homeowner's policy and you add a rental component (anything from renting a room to adding an apartment), this will have a bearing on your insurance premium. Even though it is owner occupied, it still increases the risk.

Don't rely on your lender to tell you what you need. In most cases all you need for lenders is basic, broad form fire insurance (which is basically no coverage compared to what is available).

You also shouldn't rely on your broker to tell you what you need. This is especially important recently since there are many large financial institutions that are getting into offering low-priced insurance to the masses. They often want to quote the lowest price to gain your business. However, they could accidently shortchange you on coverage. Plus they have the added pressure that if they offer too much insurance, some consumer advocacy organizations will complain that they're overselling.

I can't speak for everyone, but I will say when it comes to coverage I tend to be on the conservative side and maybe overdo it a bit (but it helps me sleep better at night). I have a personal trusted source, who I am sure I drive crazy sometimes with all my questions. His name is Ed Nix of BFL insurance brokerage.

FOURTEEN

DON'T GET ADDICTED TO DOOR COUNT

MY NAME IS MICHAEL CURRIE, AND I'M A real estate buying addict. That was me when I started out. I ran ads in the classifieds looking for properties, I had alerts from MLS set up on my phone, and I attended a monthly real estate meet-up group where I asked if anyone knew about any off-market deals. I would talk endlessly to my mortgage broker about how I could structure my next deal and read everything I could get my hands on.

The hunt excited me. My adrenalin would start to pump as soon as I found a deal. It was like a puzzle. My real estate deals would often go like this:

- ⊙ A deal is found. This creates a rush.

- ⊙ The property is looked at (possibly with competing offers). This creates another rush, along with some frustration.

- ⊙ The deal is structured for financing. This is often complicated, especially right after the mortgage crisis. Rules can change by the month, so often in fact that I would be on a race to get an approval. There are also terms and money down to think about.

- ⊙ I spend time on the phone with my insurance agent.

- ⊙ I chase people to get inspections and estimates before I sign off on conditions. This can be a frustrating time, and sometimes additional inspections are required.

- ⊙ I discuss things with my lawyer, and he always tells me to make the legal sign off the last item. He will ask me to give him time and tell me to be sure to protect myself. Many folks in the business consider this part a formality. However, I've learned it's best to give your lawyer the proper time to examine all documents.

- ⊙ A lot of factors go into the closing date. It can change several times before the deal is completed, especially if conditions must be amended. As a side note, use this as a bargaining tool. The date can provide you an upper hand when negotiating a deal. Find out what the seller wants and try to accommodate them.

- ⊙ On the actual closing day, time is money. As soon as the green light is given, it's go-time. With some projects we need to work around tenants, and of course with others, there are vacancies and are much easier. The adrenalin starts pumping like crazy on this day. The clock is set, and every day under renovation is a day without money.

- ⊙ After inevitable delays, cost overruns, change orders, and building inspector add-ons, the completion day arrives. The feeling I get here is one of relief. This is when we'll also advertise and show and screen tenants in advance so they can move in ASAP.

⊙ While it may or may not happen depending on the project, if we plan to pull out cash for the next down payment, we will have to set up a post-renovation appraisal by our mortgage broker or lender. The goal for the purchase price and renovations is to not total more than 80% of the appraised value. This will allow you to get 100% of your money out of the project (and sometimes more).

⊙ After all the hurdles, the stress, the walk close to financial ruin, the phone calls, the emails, and the victory of completion, I'll often stand outside the building, turn to my wife, and say, "Well, that wasn't so bad. What's next?" Then I do it all again.

The rush of finding a deal never goes away. I will say that now that I am more seasoned, I look for quality over quantity. I'm also a lot more focused and operate on the understanding that everything is for sale.

The process I had in the beginning was flawed in many ways. It was great for my ego, and I felt good building up my portfolio. The challenge is that it came with some major downsides. First, by going after quantity, I stepped into the world of properties in less desirable areas that consisted of a tenant base that's much harder to manage. This was based on my financial situation. I needed more units, so I had to go after cheaper properties. For example, a two-unit property in a good area could be the same price as a six-unit property in a less desirable area. I want to tread lightly on this topic, because I had many amazing lower-income tenants who looked after my units, but this wasn't always the case.

I had some tenants who seemed to find it fun to be disruptive and destroy my properties. I had never encountered these types of tenants before, so I did not budget for additional damages and the unauthorized move outs that lead to higher vacancies.

It's also true that when many tenants moved out, they left a lot of belongings behind along with garbage and damage, which ranged from sinks ripped off the wall to floors with burn marks, broken doors, and holes in the walls. Suddenly I was spread way to thin financially and could not keep up with all the maintenance and repairs. This led to more vacancies, which meant the overall quality of my portfolio was not up to the standards I imagined.

I quickly realized that it would be better to have fewer units in more desirable areas. The higher rents would allow for a better-maintained property. This strategy has led to happier tenants and a much easier portfolio to manage.

The quantity over quality investment strategy did not work out for me because it did not align with my goals as an investor. The way I approach investing now is how I pictured being a landlord would be like before I got started. I provide nice homes to nice people. I find having a small, easy-to-manage portfolio works well and is more profitable than when I had more units and more chaos to deal with on a daily basis.

FIFTEEN

THE CASH FLOW MYTH

OVER A DECADE *ago* **I STARTED ON THE** buy and hold journey. If a property appeared to have the potential for cash flow and I liked the property, I would look at the numbers with rose-coloured glasses and go all in.

The cash flow myth was the hardest concept I faced when starting out in real estate investing. I would look at a property and use a detailed spreadsheet to figure out the post-renovation rents and expenses (including vacancy rates and maintenance). I thought I knew exactly what my monthly cash flow would be. If the building worked on paper, I would go for it.

The first property I ever closed on was a side-by-side duplex. I was green, and the place was old. During the purchase process, I did a home inspection and took an electrician through the property along with my general contractor so I could begin to get the place fixed up to rent. What

I didn't check was the sewer line, and I had no idea there were tree roots growing into the sewer pipe. I moved forward with the deal and kept a tenant on one side and made the deal pending vacant possession of the other side. We took possession, fixed it up, and rented the vacant side out. The monthly cash flow for the property was a consistent $600 per month. All was good for about a year and a half. Then the sewer backed up, and one thing led to another. Insurance covered a good portion of the damage but didn't replace the sewer line.

It was quite a mess. It ended up costing us about $13,000 out of pocket, or about 21 months of cash flow in one shot. Then after three years, the roof started to leak. We had it patched, but by year four I had to replace it. That cost was $12,000—equivalent to 20 months of cash flow. You also have to keep in mind that on average, tenant turnover will cost about $900 for miscellaneous expenses like flooring and appliances.

I tell you this not to scare you but to caution you when you're buying property based on a spreadsheet. The price of great properties is likely not going to decrease anytime soon, so if you buy a fixer-upper, count on a minimum of a 10% renovation cost overrun. If you buy something a little better or new, come up with a larger down payment.

Don't make the mistakes I did. Often, I'd put as little down as possible, fix it up for as cheap as possible, maximize rent, and coast. But this strategy could end up costing you in the long run. The best piece of advice I can give you is to take the rose-coloured glasses off when looking at major components of a property, such as the roof, electrical, heating, cooling, and windows. You need to be realistic. If you think a roof will last 10 years, plan for a replacement after five. Everything has a usable life. You need to plan and have a contingency fund for the "unexpected." The reason I put that in quotes is because the one thing you can expect is the unexpected.

While this might sound like a lot of bad news, do take comfort in knowing that as you invest in properties, it gets better. If the electrical, plumbing, roof, HVAC, and insulation are good, most of the other stuff is relatively cheap and should fit within your maintenance and repair budget from your spreadsheet.

After talking to many other investors over the years, I know my story is not unique. But after reading a lot about real estate investing and listening to gurus talk about cash flow, I thought I must be doing something wrong. Rest assured, it is a common problem to face when you're just starting out. That's why it's best to be conservative on your cash flow estimates.

SIXTEEN

LOCATION

CAN YOU MAKE MONEY WITHOUT BEING IN THE perfect location?

The Starbucks theory is something that was talked about during some of my early real estate group meetings. The theory is that these types of companies do a pile of market research before they open a store. This helps them to predict that an area with one of these stores is likely either in a currently solid growing area or an area that is about to boom.[16]

As you can imagine, I was so excited when a Starbucks moved into an up-and-coming area I was investing it. I thought, Wow, I must be a real estate genius! I'd seen exactly what all these marketing and research folks saw. But then a couple of years later, Starbucks closed the location.

Does that mean the area sucks now? Nope. A quick Google search will produce many articles (some with conflicting viewpoints) about the hundreds of stores Starbucks opens and closes in any given year.

So where does that leave you? Well, I'm hoping to make you think a bit more broadly than the usual tip to buy in an up-and-coming area and easily get rich. The good news is rental properties are everywhere: small towns, large cities, rural areas, urban areas, and rentals can be had in all parts of the country. The challenge when it comes to being a landlord is the decisions you will make about the types of properties you will own and the type of residential real estate you want to get into.

So, if you want to rent a residential unit (like a room) or build an apartment building, you can. However, you need to know the reason for the rental demand, the demographics, and the overall economy of that area. For starters, renters tend to rent based on location first and economic situation second. Which prompts the question: what should you look for in an area?

Well, that depends on the kind of accommodation you want to provide. Remember, a rental market exists everywhere, and for several reasons. Here are some of the main points to remember when looking at the economy of an area:

- ⊙ What do people do in your area to make a living?

- ⊙ Do people travel for their occupation?

- ⊙ Do people move here for education?

- ⊙ Do people move here for specific work, like mining?

- ⊙ What is the average wage?

- ⊙ Is the vacancy rate high or low?

- ⊙ Do most people prefer to buy or rent?

- ⊙ Are there any major institutions such as schools, hospitals, factories, or call centres?

- ⊙ Is the area driven by natural resources, like forestry or mining?

Family Status

In my province, we have several farms that hire temporary, foreign workers for picking fruit and harvesting crops. Most of these farms provide accommodations; however, some may choose to rent a room in a local house for some or all of their stay. We also have areas that are popular fishing destinations, and people will travel to the area and live there for several months. Generally, they want a room in a house since they often go home to their families on weekends.

In other areas, we have people who work in oil fields and commute to work. With so many on and off days consisting of a work schedule that requires two weeks working followed by two weeks off, they may need temporary accommodations too.

Other types of short-term accommodations in recent years have become super popular. Tech companies such as Airbnb have made the concept of short-term accommodation easy and, in some cases, less expensive than renting a hotel room for two weeks. The rental term can range from one night to several months, and the space can be anything from the living room couch in an apartment to a luxury home.

Seniors, Singles, Couples, Families, and Pets

Housing our aging population in Canada has been a topic of conversation for many years. The Canadian government has studied the topic and recently presented some findings.[17]

Here are a few highlights:

- Seniors are the fastest growing age group in Canada.

- Seniors require diverse living arrangements and housing needs.

- It's often difficult for seniors to find affordable housing that meets all their needs.

- Most senior-led households are owned.

Elderly people have various needs. Many want to stay in communities they are familiar with. However, they often are forced to move out of their homes and move to new communities that have proper accommodations for them. I've noticed in the past several years that more and more accommodations for the people in this demographic are being built in rural areas of the country.

There are also more and more people who are looking after their elderly parents,[18] which creates a couple of opportunities. These include:

- Renting a house that has an in-law suite or second unit. A family may rent the whole thing.

- Respite care, which provides a short-term room to provide a break for people who are looking after their elderly parents.

Here are other types of renters you'll need to consider when looking at potential properties, as well as their basic needs:

- *Students*: They rent basically every type of accommodation, usually based on personal economic circumstances.

- *Work terms*: Many people require shorter-term accommodation when they need to go to an area for short-term work, which could be construction, the oil field, agriculture, medicine, etc.

- *Single people*: Often single people will seek out cheaper accommodations rather than renting a full house or apartment for one person.

- *Families*: Families always need places to live. It's often harder to find nice, affordable housing when you're a family. Families also want to be close to good schools and activity amenities, such as community pools and recreation centres. And of course, families look for easy access to grocery stores, hairdressers, and clothing stores.

- *Pet friendly*: People love their pets, so much so that they will often risk being homeless to keep them. Providing pet-friendly accommodations can get you a premium. You get bonus points if you're close to a dog park or doggy daycare.

Okay, now that you have identified the type of potential renters in your area, how do you attract them?

First, ask yourself why they would rent from you. Then ask how you can maximize your return based on your location. The best return will usually be a furnished, daily rental (but also requires the most work). The reason it requires the most work is because it needs to be cleaned frequently (possibly daily). The furniture needs to be up to a nice hotel standard. You will also have interactions with many people with various personalities and expectations, so a more hands-on management approach will be required.

You'll also need to decide what's best for you. For example, we have two private, furnished suites we rent out. However, what my wife and I find best is to rent in four-month minimum terms. We're close to a major university, so we find this works best for us to get a great return with a limited amount of work.

You can increase revenue by renting by the room in student-saturated markets. We also have other properties that are managed by a property management company, and they do traditional longer-term, unfurnished rental agreements. Shorter-term rentals with nicely furnished units will increase revenue.

This might sound easy, but it can be difficult depending on the area's zoning. In my area, most homes cannot have more than five unrelated people on the same lease. So, even if you have a six-bedroom house, you can only rent to five students.

Zoning is a complex topic since it's handled by local municipal governments. It would be great if it was standardized for a whole country, but then again that would not prevent the confusion since you can have three parallel streets that each require different zoning based on the needs and desires of the community.

For example, if you lived in a 100% single-family residential area, you would likely not want a high-rise built next to you. But you might want to be allowed to have a secondary suite.

Some common zonings include:

- Residential

- Commercial

- Industrial

- Agricultural

Then each will have a subsection based on the specific area and approved use. Here's what it looks like in my city:

- ⊙ R1 = Single-family residential unit.

- ⊙ R2 = Includes buildings with up to four units. Semidetached houses and duplex dwellings are most common. Everything covered under R1 is included as well.

The quality and condition of your units are also things to pay close attention to. Generally, you will want to be competitive, so check out rental ads around you. Aim to be better than your competition, and you shouldn't have a problem finding good renters.

Here are some tips you can use when considering the condition of one of your units:

- ⊙ Do not over-renovate or under-renovate.

- ⊙ Check out current trends. You should also look for less expensive versions of items that tend to be pricey.

- ⊙ Many people use quartz instead of granite for countertops.

- ⊙ If you're in an area with regular laminate countertops, buy a high-end version. (It won't cost much more, but it will look way better.)

- ⊙ Backsplashes with simple white tile can add a lot of value to a kitchen with minimal expense.

- ⊙ Laminate or bamboo floors can be a great alternative to hardwood.

If you're renting in a high-end area and charging a high rent price, then don't scrimp on the details. The finest materials will help your client rationalize your rental rate. If you ever get a tour of a high-end home, you will notice the agent will always make a point of pointing out things like Italian tile directly imported from a certain region of Italy and those types of things.

To summarize, you'll want to determine who would want to rent from you and then plan to attract and retain them. In a hot rental market, it could be easy. However, take it from somebody who has been in the game for a while—times are not always good.

Back in 2011, I can remember my wife, Shelly, and I trying to rent a flat and didn't get any good-quality applicants. We even did an open house on a Sunday afternoon. We were patient and never let our guard down. We followed our screening process, and after a couple of months having a vacant unit, we finally found a great tenant.

RENT A ROOM

I HEARD *what* SOUNDED LIKE A PARTY, SO I knocked on the door. Sure enough, the new tenant in our home had friends over, and they were smoking the good stuff. When the tenant began to give off the vibe that he owned the place, I reminded him of our no-guest and no-smoking policies. I asked him to get everyone out and informed him I would speak to him in the morning.

He denied that anyone was smoking but obviously could not deny the guests. The next day I called him and pointed out that our setup might not be the right fit and told him that if he would move out immediately, I would give him back his money—including the damage deposit.

I'm not sure why he took the room in the first place, but I was happy he agreed and left without any tenancy board hassle.

The idea of taking in boarders is likely one of the oldest forms of landlording. It's simple, as people often migrate to areas for work or school. They're generally looking for a clean bed, shower, short-term lease, and a reasonable price. I've talked to some people who have also provided bag lunches and other meals for an additional charge. Luckily, the process of renting a room in your home is simple.

Place an ad, set the expectations of what space they can occupy, make it clear what they have access to, screen them, and sign a lease. One major point of emphasis here is to make sure they comply with your current landlord agreement (if you are doing in it a home you are renting), follow your city's regulations, and have the proper insurance in place.

You will need to use a proper screening process that includes a credit application. It is also important to clearly lay out exactly what the expectations and restrictions are. A best practice for screening your tenants is as follows:

- Send an application.

- Do a credit check.

- Require current and previous landlord references.

- Ask for a personal reference.

- Include some form of income verification.

You can also include other rules to follow, like no lying on the couch, no strangers in the room, no "relations" in the room, no dirty dishes on the counter or sink, no smoking (all substances), no visitors (or visitor rules), and single occupancy only. (You would be amazed at how many people try to sneak or add people to a single-room arrangement.) You can specify restrictions on common areas, such as the room only, plus bathroom, whether or not you will allow access to laundry facilities, and if so, what will the rules be. (Think time of day and laundry left in the washer or dryer.) You can even add details on the room temperature.

My wife, Shelly, and I took over a home one time with agreements in place for rented suites. When we read the room agreements, we thought it seemed harsh, but it didn't take us long to realize why all those rules were in place. Communication, clarity, and accountability are the best ways to run an operation when you're renting out space in your home. And if you do it right, it's probably the easiest way to make cash right away in real estate.

HOUSE HACKING

I missed out on thousands of dollars in revenue for several years by not getting into house hacking earlier. Do not let that happen to you, and start as soon as you can.

In its basic form, house hacking is all about buying a property, living in part of it, and renting out the rest. This can mean anything from renting a room to renting out several separate units on your property. The term was popularized by Brandon Turner of Biggerpockets.com and has become commonplace in the real estate investing community. I highly recommend that aspiring real estate investors try out a version of this technique.

Before we got into buy and hold investing, Shelly and I looked at some two-unit properties as an option for us to live in. We were not sold on the idea of having another family or person sharing space in our home. Then we put our personal home up for sale, and part of the deal was a quick closing. That meant we needed to find a place to live fast. At the same time, we were closing on a two-unit investment property with a vacant unit upon possession.

We decided to move into the unit to give us time to find a place of our own. (I mean, we figured we would make good tenants.) Here is the interesting, life-changing part: There was a family of four living in the lower unit, and we shared a driveway. We figured we would hear them all the time, but as time went on, we were surprised by how quiet it was and how little we saw of them. They felt more like neighbours than tenants. This experience changed our search parameters from looking for a single-family home to looking for a single-family home with a rental component.

House hacking changed our financial lives. The tax benefits were incredible, plus the income helped reduce our monthly overhead, allowing us to save more money and buy more properties. If I could go back in time, I would have bought a house at a much younger age and rented rooms or a basement suite, or even bought a three- or four-unit building where I could live in one unit and rent out the others.

Currently we have a family home with two rental suites attached to it. They have private entrances and are furnished. We rent in shorter terms, mostly four months at a time since we are in a university district. Our process for tenant selection is extremely thorough, so it allows us an easy way to make monthly income with minimal effort. The income and the tax benefits outweigh any hassles or perceived hassles that might come up.

NINETEEN

THE BASEMENT SUITE

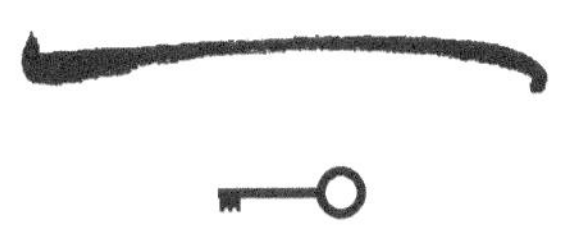

THIS FITS IN LINE *with* THE PREVIOUS CHAPTER on house hacking, and the story in the previous chapter was our first experience with a literal basement suite. The term has broadened in recent times with a new movement of folks building backyard suites, or like us, back in late 2010, we found a great old house with plenty of character. The biggest selling point for us was the two-bedroom, top-floor apartment.

We have always had great tenants, which I am sure made a big difference. It also made us realize that we'd been missing out on one of the greatest and easiest real estate investment opportunities available.

Do you want to maximize your earning potential? What would you do to earn an extra week's worth of pay every month? Did you know there could be tax advantages to having part of your home rented? It's a strategy so simple that we did not see it. Every property we've purchased since that experience back in 2009 has had a rental component. We soon discovered some additional financial advantages at tax time. (You will need to check on the tax laws in your area.) It was one of those ah-ha moments.

When I speak with first-time home buyers, as well as those who want to invest in real estate, I tell them this story. I also point out how simple building wealth through investing in real estate can be.

My friend, fellow real estate investor, and coach Mike Burgess says it best in Sunil Tulsiani and Brian Tracy's book, *The Secret to Wealth*. "I chose to share my home with a tenant rather than try and find a fifth week in each month," and "building a rental suite in your house will not make you wealthy, but it can be an important component in achieving your goals."[19]

You can buy an existing multifamily property or build additional value for a property by adding a suite. Keep in mind that you will need to check local zoning bylaws as well as building code rules to make sure it's feasible. There are also some challenges to be aware of, especially with basement suites, which can be difficult or very expensive. Some examples would be ceiling height requirements, square footage requirement, and bedroom window egress requirements.

If your property meets all the building requirements, there are several ways to add a suite to a property. The most common is a basement apartment, but don't rule out building up, off the back, or even on top of a detached garage. You can add significant value to a home by adding a suite, especially in this era of families looking after elderly parents who may want a home with an in-law suite. Of course, the growing popularity of Airbnb or similar types of short-term rental models also make this an option to earn income.

Here are a few pros and cons to consider:

PROS

- ⊙ Additional income may cover part or all of your mortgage payment.

- ⊙ It will allow for quicker equity building. This could be accelerated if you were to save the additional monthly income and make an annual lump sum payment with the rental income.

- ⊙ There are numerous potential tax benefits.

- ⊙ You will see an increase in the value of your home when you sell, especially if you sell it with an existing tenant and a well-documented steady revenue.

- ⊙ There are additional increases to be had in the value of your home if you add one or more rental suites.

CONS

- ⊙ You will reduce the personal usable space in your home. If you build a basement apartment, you may lose significant living space.

- ⊙ You will give up privacy. It's inevitable that you'll cross paths with your tenants at some point.

- ⊙ You'll have to deal with more noise at inconvenient times. Shelly and I would never say we are the quietest family around. Noise irritation can work both ways, and when the tenant is your paying customer, you may need to adjust the volume of your family's daily activities.

- ⊙ Neighbours may not always share in your excitement about adding a rental component to your home. You will need to be aware of any neighbours who oppose your idea of adding a rental suite. If you buy a home with an existing rental suite, this will not likely be a problem.

⊙ You will become a 24/7 landlord and property manager. You'll need to set boundaries up front so that you're not getting a knock on the door at 2 a.m. for a nonemergency repair.

20% DOWN

IS IT CRAZY TO PUT 20% OR MORE down on a property? While it might seem like a crazy idea to some, putting 20% or more down when you purchase a property is the easiest way to begin investing in real estate.

Even though there are many strategies when it comes to investing in real estate, this is one that never seems to get a lot of press. Maybe it is too boring, but I like this simple approach. In my area you are required to have a 20% down payment to purchase a noncommercial, multifamily income property. That generally means a residential property up to five units. If you have the 20% down payment from savings, it will benefit you in several ways:

⊙ You'll have better odds of getting a lower or preferred interest rate at the bank.

- ⊙ You may avoid paying CMHC (Canada Mortgage and Housing Commission) fees that are required on high-leverage mortgages in Canada.[20]

- ⊙ You'll decrease your total amount to finance, which may allow you to shorten the term and pay it off quicker.

- ⊙ You'll reduce the amount of interest you pay.

- ⊙ Paying your mortgage off quicker means you can reduce your debt-service ratio. Lenders like when you have lower debt compared to your income level.

- ⊙ You'll decrease your amount to finance, so you can take the mortgage over the maximum allowable term and increase your monthly cash flow.

- ⊙ It'll likely put you in an equity position from day number one.

- ⊙ It's a less stressful way to invest. You have better odds of being welcomed with open arms when you walk into the bank.

- ⊙ Having higher cash flow can lead to less stress when it comes to finding money for maintenance and repairs.

I'm not going to get into the disadvantages here. It comes down to a choice based on your investment strategy. What I have noticed over my investing career is that people seem to talk a lot about the big gains, zero-down, and refinance strategies to line your pockets. I do not see very much written about the people who put 20%, 50%, or 75% down on properties and pay them off quickly and retire on the cash flow. I've often heard people in various real estate meetings being ridiculed for even suggesting the idea. Whatever you decide to do, come up with a plan, and make it work. Do what works best for you and your situation.

Here's how you can keep it simple and put 20% down on your investment property. First, you'll need to save up a down payment. This is a common way for people to purchase a rental property. The amount down will depend on local mortgage rules, the buyer's credit rating, and the type and size of the property. If you want to get into real estate investing in a low-risk way, then save up 20% down and then buy a two- to four-unit property in good condition located in a desirable area. Hire a good property manager and presto—you'll be on your way to gaining wealth in real estate. All you'll have to do from there is save and repeat. It may take you longer, but if you plan on working your regular job until retirement age, why complicate the process? This simple method is often referred to as buy and hold investing.

The down payment can be even greater than 20% too, and this can often allow you to get better rates and terms from lenders. In addition, it will improve the property's cash flow, giving you more money each month to pay down the mortgage, renovate, or live off the money you're making on the property. You can even shorten the mortgage term and pay your property off quicker. This is a strategy that's often contrary to what you might read about but can be a very easy way to build wealth over time.

Most Challenging Project Before Pic (back of Barton House)

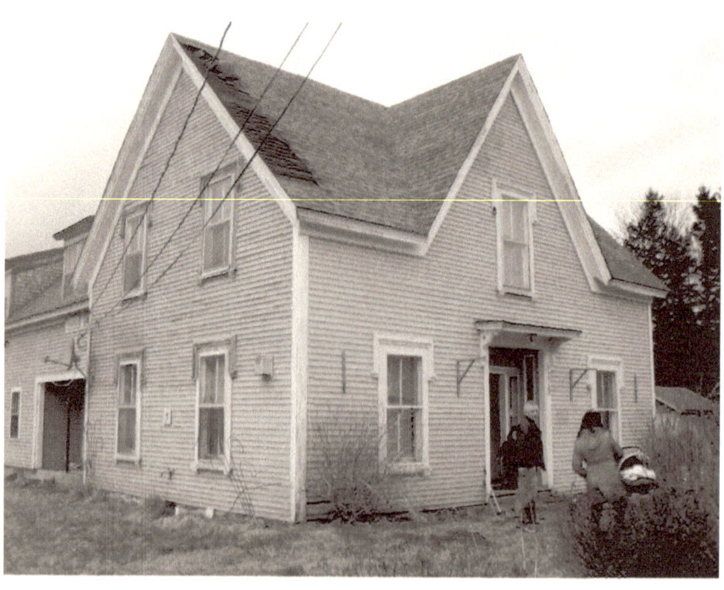

Most Challenging Project Before Pic (front of Barton House)

Most Challenging Project After Pic (back of Barton House)

Most Challenging Project After Pic (front of Barton House)

Most Terrifying Electrical Set Up I Have Ever Seen on a 4-plex I Purchased
Note: the leaking sewage pipe over head

My First Income Property (two units, 3 bed up & 2 Bed down)

AIRBNB

THIS PAST SUMMER, *my* FRIEND INVITED MY FAMILY to visit at an Airbnb property he was staying in with his family. The house was not that big but was a well put-together, tastefully renovated old house in a seaside community just outside of Halifax that offered an attractive getaway. It got me thinking. Between the internet and the staycation movement, some really unique opportunities have become available. Back in the '70s when we travelled as a family, we would stay at nationally branded hotels like Howard Johnson or something similar, and our only criterion as kids was that it must have a pool. Renting some stranger's house in a rural area wasn't even an option.

Back then, that would have been just weird. Jamming ourselves into a small hotel room seemed like a much better option. Today though, many houses in rural areas are vacant or used very infrequently as cottages. Now they're getting filled with families, which is a much better use of these old houses. This could even be saving some small towns.

Can you remember how the whole Airbnb phenomenon started? Well, it started off as something totally different and was more about letting someone sleep on your couch or in a spare room.[21] Eventually it evolved into what you see today, and it can be a great way to make money on an investment property.

Fortunately, there are great screening platforms to keep it safe too. With the Airbnb business model, the possibilities are endless. It could be that you have a spare room, a part of a house (such as a finished basement), a cottage, or home you do not occupy all the time.

Currently, we're dealing with a national pandemic. Canada requires a 14-day quarantine period when someone enters the country, unless they're fully vaccinated.[22] This has also created a unique business opportunity for those with rooms or apartments with a private entrance.[23] I have a friend who has made good money renting to people in quarantine despite the fact the travel industry has been decimated. She adds value for the guests by shopping for them, helping them learn about the various restaurants that deliver, and teaching them how to use apps like Uber Eats.

You don't have to be in a pandemic to find opportunity. Location, cleanliness, flexibility on price, and length of stay are all important factors that can help you create a successful rental property. I know an industry leader and Airbnb specialist who has built a very successful business without owning a bunch of properties. His name is Sid Kosatsky.

Sid uses the Airbnb site and his own site named Hostoften.com. He handles the bookings for his clients' properties and charges a fee of part of the revenue to manage the property. He has different levels of management depending on the owner:

- *International properties*: This is online management, with a fee of 20% total revenue and is available worldwide.

  - Remote management solution
  - Create online listings
  - 24/7 guest communications
  - Inquiry and calendar management
  - Coordinate with local teams
  - Dispatch maintenance personnel
  - Enforce rules
  - Interact with Airbnb resolution team
  - Detailed financial reporting

- *Full-service property management*: 25% rental revenue

  - Available in Nova Scotia
  - Ideal for homeowners and investors
  - Professional photographs
  - Design advice
  - 24/7 guest communications
  - Inquiry and calendar management
  - Provide local property management
  - Schedule and supervise cleaners
  - Restock and inspect
  - Dispatch maintenance personnel
  - Enforce rules
  - Interact with Airbnb resolution team
  - Detailed financial reporting

⊙ *Airbnb cleaning*: Stand-alone service with an $85+ charge for each visit

- Available in Nova Scotia
- Cleaning service as a stand-alone service
- Flat-rate pricing set to your listing
- Takes pictures of service
- Inspects property
- Notifies if damage is discovered
- Sets up property in time for guests
- Thoroughly checks for cleanliness

He has a fully staffed Airbnb cleaning company. The cool part is that this company can deploy at a moment's notice and switch out the sheets and towels when needed. They set up each Airbnb with the same sheets, towels, cutlery, dishes, and curtains, which makes for a quick switch. He charges a cleaning fee for every stay and charges about $100.

One of the cool parts of his company is the inventory. Along with regular owners, he approaches developers who have condos or apartments that are in the process of selling or renting. He offers a monthly rent and a specified lease term that's a bit above market. He then furnishes the unit and rents it out. If you do this, you need to make sure you are properly insured and that it's legal in the building based on condominium board rules and local bylaws.

It's a win-win, as the developer or property owner gets a premium guaranteed rent, and Sid gets an Airbnb unit for the cost of furniture. In addition to this formula, Sid also manages Airbnbs for other people. It can be a lot of work to constantly turn units, so he takes a cut of the gross rent in return for setting up the guests and arranging the cleaning.

If you're considering an Airbnb or any short-term rental model, make sure to have a proper screening process. Unfortunately, unlike with a traditional rental property, you will need to use a different process for screening your Airbnb tenants. You will also have to trust that most of your guests will be great. If you make your listing too restrictive you may miss out on some great guests and limit your listings appeal.

The most common risks for Airbnbs are as follows:

- Parties
- Rule violations
- Additional guests
- Potential property damage
- Fraud or criminal activity
- Prostitution
- Drug dealing
- Junkie dens
- Fake bookings or stolen listings
- Identity theft

Because of the risks, communication with your guests is key. Don't be so excited to rent your space that you forget to ask basic screening questions and reiterate the rules of your rental. Rules could include things like no parties, no smoking, and quiet times. Set up security cameras pointing at entry doors, and let the guest know the cameras are there for their protection. Ask questions prior to the booking like the following:

⊙ *What is the purpose of your stay?* If they say a bachelorette party, make sure to reiterate you do not allow parties and have a late-night noise restriction.

⊙ *How many people will be staying with you?* This will indicate who will be there and provide the opportunity to talk about additional charges for more guests.

⊙ *Where are you travelling from?* This will let you know if they are tourist travellers, or people looking for a cool spot to have a party. Many local people might rent your space, especially in this era of staycations.

   • *Have you stayed at an Airbnb before?* If they have stayed at many, they will likely also have a rating. Keep in mind a person with a low rating may get a friend to handle the booking.

   • *Do you smoke?* Most places are nonsmoking. This will give you the opportunity to be clear about your non-smoking policy. Make sure to include "all substances."

   • *Do you have any pets?* Even if your place is pet-free, folks might sneak in a pet, but simply asking them if they have a pet will make them think twice.

Unfortunately, simply asking questions will not always protect you. It's a simple situation where a popular Airbnb on a daily rate can generate way more revenue than the same space as a long-term rental, so with the risk comes potential for a great reward. You will need to make sure that you, as the landlord, understand the rules and regulations in your area. This includes reporting your income properly or any required property registration. Also make sure to have the proper insurance to cover your operation.

Bed-and-Breakfast

About 20 years ago, long before I got into buy and hold real estate investing, I did business with a guy who invited me over to his house to pick up a motorcycle I was buying from him. It was summertime, and when I showed up, I found him in the camper on a vacant lot next to his house. This was the first time I got an up close and personal introduction to the bed-and-breakfast business model.

I could not help but ask a bunch of questions. He explained how for six months of the year his wife would rent out all the bedrooms in their house, and they would live in a camper on the lot next door. The location was just outside the city. He did not have a huge house, and it wasn't what you might picture as a bed-and-breakfast. It was a split-entry bungalow about 10 years old with three bedrooms upstairs and two downstairs.

He explained how it wasn't necessarily a huge money maker, but his wife loved greeting guests and making breakfast for travellers from all over the globe. It also came with a lot of great tax benefits. Today I can't help but think how Airbnb would have enhanced the way they operated. I can also remember thinking I was not sold on the idea of having people living in my house while I lived in a camper. However, they were empty nesters, they loved doing it, and it really worked for them. It might work for you.

Airbnb has streamlined the conventional bed-and-breakfast business model, but the one I am referring to in this book is the classic model. It's quite simple. You rent rooms in your home based on a daily rate and allow guests to have the use of common areas such as a living room and provide them with breakfast in the morning.

There are many benefits to running a bed-and-breakfast. It's an allowable use of an owner-occupied home in many areas. You will need to check with local regulations and apply to be officially designated. You may have to do some fire- and safety-related upgrades to your home and have proper insurance before you get started.

Here are some of the benefits:

- You can operate in your own home. Now with modern technology like doors with keypads, you don't necessarily have to be home to greet guests.

- You can expense most of your operating costs and live for free. (Make sure to check with a tax accountant who is familiar with the tax laws in your area.)

- You can meet people from all over the world.

- You can make a name for yourself in the culinary world if you enjoy cooking for people. This is a great way to be able to provide daily meals.

- You get to decide when you take guests. Many people will operate seasonally and take the rest of the year off. If you live in a colder climate, you may want to take the winter off.

- You can earn money by offering additional services, such as canoe or kayak rentals and guided tours for things like hiking, diving, or sailing.

The other great part is that you can decide if you want to provide a full breakfast, continental breakfast, or even coupons to a local restaurant. Our current home is a previous bed-and-breakfast. It was purpose renovated, so it has six bedrooms, each with their own full bath. Each room is like an individual, private suite.

We may open it back up as a full bed-and-breakfast in the future. However, in the short term, we're renting two of the suites that have outside entrances. We do not serve breakfast, and our shortest term is four months (since we are in a university area). This has provided a low-maintenance, easy-to-run operation for us. We have very limited interaction with our tenants, though I do love learning their stories and have even had some come back to stay with us when they're in Canada.

Now some things to consider:

- *Insurance*: Since you're allowing multiple short-term guests in your home, the risk can be considered high, so make sure to factor that in.

- *Property tax increase*: Depending on where you're located, you may be subject to pay a higher property tax.

- *Neighbours*: Although a bed-and-breakfast property is ok from a zoning point of view in many areas, it does not mean your neighbours are going to be in love with the idea—especially if your guests are loud or park in front of their houses. Consider the layout of the area before you purchase a home and open it up as a bed and breakfast.

- *Privacy and security*: Since this is generally run as a hands-on business in your home, if you have rooms booked, you are on stage. Also, since they are short term, it will be unlikely that you will have the opportunity to do a background check on every guest. That means the safety of you and your family could be at risk. I don't want to scare you, but it's something you'll want to consider.

TWENTY-TWO

INTERNATIONAL STUDENTS

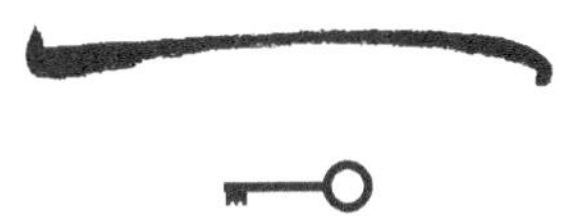

THIS IS ~~not~~ MY STORY. HOWEVER, I FOUND an established, active host who has been taking in international students for over a decade. We'll call her Barb. Barb's experiences have been positive. She got into hosting international students when a friend of hers talked about her own experience. Barb, who lived alone, liked the sound of having someone around to care for, so she contacted an association that teaches English language skills to international students in her city. They arranged her first student.

The organization charges an all-inclusive fee for the student to come study in Canada. Then they pay the homestay host market rent and board. Barb also loves to cook for and feed her students but has to be careful with the food budget so they don't eat up all the profits. Some students want to shop for their own food, and Barb has made deals with some for a rent reduction to compensate them for groceries.

She said some of her students previously stayed in places that were dirty, crowded, or lacked food. There was one case she remembered where the host placed a plate with some crackers and a piece of cheese in front of the student and said if they want to eat more than that, they need to pay more money.

The length of stay can vary, so it's a great way to get an influx of cash over what could be just a one- to two-month stay. Sometimes the students just want to try out the country for a month, and other times they may want to move to a different location to see what it's like. Barb said she forms relationships with her students. They all call her Mom, and through Skype or FaceTime, she often meets parents and other family members.

She has had students from Korea, Saudi Arabia, and India. The initial goal for many is to first learn English by taking English classes and being immersed in the English language. Then they apply for university or other postsecondary education. The backgrounds vary, and the services hosts are required to provide depend on the agency.

For example, many require you to help the students with paperwork, making sure they have their medical insurance set up as well as taking them on tours to show them where the school they're attending is located. They may also want to know the bus routes, get help with setting up a bank account, and other necessities.

What are the potential downfalls? Well, when I conducted my interview, Barb said although her experiences were positive, she has spoken to other folks who have had negative experiences. Some of the students are 18 to 19 years old and without family influence in a foreign country. (That in its own sounds dangerous.) Sometimes a student boarder may stay out late and leave you worried about where they might be. One student snuck a person in late at night. Others have brought friends over while the hosts were away.

In many cases, the rent is being paid by the student directly, and if they don't pay, you end up chasing rent in your own home. In another case, one of her student guests started skipping school, and the school clawed back on the direct rent payment, stating that it was the host's responsibility to get them to go to school.

You must set rules and be extremely clear on boundaries, such as if they can have friends over and when, if at all. Barb suggests making a strict rule about not allowing intimate relations to happen in the room or apartment. She also recommended creating rules stating no parties or gatherings. She said it's relatively easy to find a homestay organization with a quick Google search. The price you receive for room and board will be based on market rent (which is different in all areas). Like any other rental ad, you will send pictures of what you offer as well as your location and proximity to language schools and other educational institutions.

Barb shared a lot of insight and really opened my eyes to an interesting way to become a real estate investor. It's a great option if you genuinely want to create a great experience for a young person from another country. The money earned is intended to cover the cost of the room and board, but many families find there is additional money left over after monthly expenses are paid.

There are many opportunities and agencies around the globe that will pair you with a student and pay you to board and feed them for one year. This is an amazing way to learn about another culture and teach your children about other cultures. If you Google homestay hosts, hosting foreign exchange students, or homestay international, you will find many options.

The amount of money you will receive depends on the agency, country, services you offer, age of the student, and length of stay. Can you make money? The cost of entry is basically zero. You just need a spare room. You can get started almost immediately, and you can bring a lot of value to a young person's life. The amount of money you make or do not make will also come down to the agency you use and, of course, the food and experiences you provide.

TWENTY-THREE

STUDENT HOUSING

MY FRIEND RECEIVED A *call* ON A FRIDAY night at around 9:00 p.m. He had just set up his tenants in a student rental property he had. The caller was a young woman attending a university in the area. (She had just moved in.) She asked if he could bring over some toilet paper because they were almost out. He was a bit taken aback by the question. He let her know that she and the other roommates were responsible for their own toilet paper.

The caller was a bit frustrated and said, "You told me this was an all-inclusive rental."

If you live near any postsecondary (and in some cases high school) institutions, you will have demand for student housing. I want to share with you a way to make money with student housing as a real estate investing option.

The most common method or what most people think of when they hear the term "student housing investing" is when you buy a whole house or small multifamily property (generally one to four units) and rent it by the room. Renting by the room is a great way to increase the revenue of an apartment or house. You will have to weigh the pros and cons. What I have come to realize in real estate investing is that when you do something to increase revenue, it will come at a cost. Student housing has many challenges. The most important thing you can do is set expectations when you sign the lease. Make sure to carefully list what is or isn't included. Set the expectations on the cleanliness of the room and common areas, for personal space, and what's expected for noise levels or quiet times. If the tenant is required to pay a portion of any bills for heat, electricity, internet, food, etc., they need to know up front.

Here are some of the positive aspects of renting rooms to students:

- ⊙ *More revenue*: You'll have an opportunity to increase the revenue of the property.

- ⊙ *Paid rent*: Students don't typically miss rent, and even if they do, you can get parents to co-sign. In some cases, students like to pay several months in advance. I do want to note that sometimes if a student drops out, they may leave town and skip out on rent.

- ⊙ *Coin-operated laundry*: If you have a property rented by the room, a great way to make additional cash is to install a coin-operated washer and dryer. If you do not want the hassle of repairs, maintenance, or vandalism (which happens when people try to steal the coins), there are companies that will work out a deal with you, where they take care of the machines (maintenance and money collection) and share the proceeds with you.

- *Annual lease*: When you have student rentals on an annual lease, you can charge for the full 12 months and require the student to pay for the entire length of their stay. When students aren't in town, you can do Airbnb or similar services for the other months.

- *Low vacancy*: The vacancy rate for student housing is generally very low, although it has risen over course of the pandemic.[24]

- *Parent co-signers*: You can ask parents to co-sign the lease for a student. I have a friend who runs several student properties. He requires a credit card to be left on file. He makes sure the parents know that they will be liable for any damage done by the student.

Here are some of the negative aspects to renting to students by the room:

- *Higher property management expenses*: You'll find that property managers charge more to manage student housing. This is because it takes more time and emotional energy to manage a student property. This can be due to personality conflicts between tenants, tenants failing school, and tenants abandoning the property.

- *Common-area cleaning*: You will need to hire a cleaner to make sure common areas and bathrooms are clean. Having your tenants arrange their own cleaning schedule will likely end in a dispute. You will also need someone to take care of the garbage removal, lawn care, and snow cleanup. The cleaner can also be your eyes on the ground.

- *Higher maintenance costs*: When you rent to multiple people, it can be hard on a property. This may include higher appliance repair costs, as well as broken cupboard doors, window screens, flooring, and problems with things like plumbing.

⊙ *Utilities paid by the landlord*: You will need to pay the utilities or rely on your tenants to make sure they are paid. I would recommend paying them yourself to ensure they are all paid on time. This will include a Wi-Fi bill.

⊙ *Higher insurance costs*: Insurance companies consider houses set up like rooming houses to be a higher risk for bad things to happen. It's important to get a quote and factor in the cost of insurance before you buy a student property.

⊙ *Government regulation*: Many areas put limits on student properties. In my area, no matter what size the house is, you can only rent to five unrelated people per unit. This was changed many years ago, because what some landlords were doing was buying a set of flats and then turning every closet, dining room, and living room into a rentable bedroom. In the end many of these two-unit properties would have up to 18 rooms (nine per unit). This created lots of cash flow. However, they were not popular with the neighbours.

⊙ *Local zoning and bylaws:* If a house is considered a rooming house, it may fall into a different category of zoning, which may make it illegal to operate.[25] In many areas, you can only have one lease per unit. This means in order to have more than one student in a unit, you may have to make a custom lease, or add to the lease. If the lease is not compliant, you may be in violation of local tenancy rules. All investors need to do their due diligence. I have seen some big old houses for sale next to universities, and they might advertise 10 rooms for rent. The challenge is that if you buy the house based on the cash flow of 10 rooms, and then the local government says you can only rent five of them, you could be in a lot of financial trouble if you already purchased the property. Zoning bylaws become a problem if you poorly manage your student property too. It will usually be a neighbour who makes a complaint to the local bylaw office. The other part of bylaw compliance might have to do with the kind of appliances, if any, you can have in a room. You may be allowed to have a fridge and a microwave, but in many areas, as soon as you add a range it is considered an additional unit.

- *Fire and building code requirements*: If you set up a property that acts like a rooming house, you will have to check local building code and fire regulations. This might include certain fire separation requirements such as solid doors or metal-covered doors on the bedrooms. It could also include a certain number of fire extinguishers, solid ceilings (not drop ceilings), occupancy per square foot, bedroom requirements, and egress requirements for windows in rooms that are going to be used as bedrooms. I'm not sure where old-school hot plates fit (either under insurance risks, bylaws, or fire regulations). However, I would recommend you do not allow them in your rented rooms.

- *Housing and condominium association rules*: These organizations can put limitations on student housing. They might not necessarily discriminate against students, but they can ruin your experience as a landlord. Make sure you're allowed to rent to students before you buy a property if that's your plan.

- *Risk of out-of-control parties*: It was not long ago I saw a story on the local news about a student property in an affluent university area getting out of control. The students were yelling at police and standing on the roof above the front step. Being away from home for the first time can change a person. Add alcohol or drugs into the mix, and things can get weird. It can also be worse since many student properties are located in upscale areas around postsecondary institutions. This often means that quiet families might not be tolerant of party houses.

ELDERLY CARE

She yelled for dinner as she does every night. Only, in this house, she has a daily dinner party of 13 people, which includes seven elderly boarders (residents) and a husband with four children.

They dined together like this every night for almost 20 years. Yes, the residents would change, and of course, the children grew up and left home, but the business kept on going. While doing research, I wanted to touch on a growing area of opportunity that allows a person to work from home and do fulfilling work. There are many ways to participate, but I want to start with an inspiring story.

I had the pleasure of interviewing one of the most thoughtful and caring people I have ever met. She wanted me to change her name, so I will call her Jane. Jane ran a boardinghouse for seniors for about 20 years. She is a nurse by trade but said that's not a requirement. Her inspiration to start this kind of home came from working in health care.

She noticed when folks got old and sick, they would get stuck in the hospital for long periods of time and could not go home since they often lived alone and didn't have any family to help. Some were on a waiting list for a seniors' home, but the lists would be long, especially if they wanted to stay in the area they lived in.

Out of need, she decided she would look into opening up her home and take in elderly boarders without it becoming a fully licensed facility. In her area, the first step was verifying the zoning of her home and then finding out about all the regulations. It turned out she was able to have 10 full-time boarders—seven if they were bed ridden or required additional care due to mobility issues.

While this arrangement can be unlicensed, it can't be unregulated. The good news was that she and her husband already had a large home. The downside was they had to modify it to safely accommodate their family and residence.

The public health department in Nova Scotia made sure she had proper-size rooms, an area large enough to seat all the residents for both eating and leisure, as well as adequate staff to help. They focused on living conditions and quality of life items. For tenants who can't move, you need proper equipment to get them out of bed. It's a 24/7 operation, so you will need to have additional help. In her case, she had her husband as well as three other part-time staff.

Her business model was to provide a clean, safe home with three home-cooked meals each day. She also offered an annual birthday party that included being able to bring in up to 15 guests. She would serve tea, sandwiches, and provide a cake. It was sort of a cross between taking in regular boarders (tenants) and a nursing home. She also kept track of when to provide medication and connected tenants to local outreach groups to help improve their quality of life (local churches that would pick them up for church, or services to go shopping or visit friends).

Next of course were building code and fire marshal requirements. These included proper smoke and carbon monoxide detectors, wheelchair-accessible doors, proper egress in all windows, proper exterior walkways, and oil or electric heat only (no wood heat was permitted). Grab bars were required near toilets, tubs, and showers. Fire extinguishers, safety lights (for when the power goes out), and fire escapes from the upper floors were mandatory. The fire marshal as well as a public health official were required to complete an annual inspection.

To run this kind of business out of an investment property, you will also need a lot of insurance. The risk of your tenants having a slip-and-fall accident is quite high since you're housing them full time. Keep in mind all boardinghouse situations cost more to insure.

When I asked what she would do if she had a chance to do it all over again, without hesitation she said she would. Here is her list of pros for this type of arrangement:

- *Revenue*: You can charge a lot more per room than a regular landlord due to the additional requirements.

- *Tax benefits*: You have lots of expenses. While this can hurt your revenue stream, it can be great at tax time.

- *Work from home and be your own boss*: Earning a living at home is always a good thing.

- *Large home*: You get to live in an above average-size home.

- *Long-term tenants*: Most tenants want to live out the rest of their days in your home. The longest tenant Jane had was 10 years.

- *Healthy, home-cooked meals for you, your family, and your ten-*

ants: In fact, Jane said she made fresh bread daily as part of her routine.

- *Family involvement*: Jane made this business a family affair, with her husband and children being quite involved.

- *Fulfilling work*: You get the opportunity to hear stories and spend time with the elderly.

Below is a list of her cons for this kind of arrangement:

- *Setup can be costly*: This is especially true when compared to just renting rooms in your house to anyone.

- *Expenses*: It can be a very expense-laden business model.

- *Regulations*: These can be difficult to navigate and, at times, a bit intrusive. Building inspectors, fire marshals, and public health officials are the main ones.

- *Death*: Unfortunately, this is the main reason for vacancies.

- *Unexpected vacancy*: Unfortunately if someone dies, they can't give notice. In some cases, the family may provide some compensation, but in many cases they do not. You will want to fill your vacancy as quickly as possible, but at the same time, you will need to be sensitive to the family of the tenant who died.

- *Emotional attachment to your tenants*: Let's face it—when you eat with and clean up after your senior tenants, you become friends. The challenge is that, for the most part, these tenants come into your life when they are in their 80s.

- *Vacation time*: If you want to leave the house for more than a few hours, you'll need to plan and hire coverage. Something like a family vacation can suddenly become very expensive.

- *Turning away potential tenants based on income*: A question Jane would have to ask if a person was to stay in her home was regarding their income and ability to pay the required fees. Unfortunately, many people cannot afford this kind of care. Also, since she was not licensed, the government would not contribute.

- *Skilled labour requirements*: Although you may not have to be certified in a specific field, it helps if you are, or you will need to hire certified professionals. Jobs may include cooking, building maintenance, property management, nursing, doctors, personal care work, or accounting. Having the strength to lift people would also be a great skill.

Jane said getting boarders usually happened by word of mouth—especially if you form relationships with people who work in hospitals. They are usually the ones tasked with re-homing a patient to free up a hospital bed. She also mentioned the possibility of spin-off business opportunities such as shuttle services, personal shopping, and fun excursions.

Utilizing the facility and working with families who look after elderly parents or relatives can leave a room free to provide respite or short-term care. This could be over a weekend or for a few days or weeks to give a break to the senior's primary caregiver. During the tail end of her time running the business, there was a growing demand for senior daycare. It was like daycare for children or pets, only for seniors. This can be especially good if they live alone or with family.

Finally, you can leave a room free for hospice or palliative care. This is when a person is terminally ill but would like to die with peace and dignity. You look after them in their final days. Senior housing is a growing area of the rental business. There are some agencies out there, such as British Columbia–based Happipad, that match young folks who have been priced out of the rental market with community members.[26] In exchange for an affordable room, a young person might offer companionship to a senior, for example. This is a great option for a senior to stay in their home longer as well as earn some income.

Many homeowners currently struggle with record-high housing costs and increasing social isolation. The companion-housing initiative enables older Canadians to remain living independently, helps homeowners cut down their monthly costs, and connects compatible people to create a memorable living experience.

Joining the initiative also creates incredibly valuable housing opportunities for members of the community who are most in need, like students, immigrants, refugees, and people going through transitions in their lives. I love their business model. I mean, imagine how many lonely seniors are out there living in big houses, some of whom are also strapped for cash. It's definitely a win-win situation.

My final thoughts on elderly care facilities are that it's a fast-growing and potentially lucrative area of the residential rental market. It can be an expense-laden, high-responsibility segment, but it can be rewarding at the same time. To succeed, you'll need to focus on systems so it doesn't consume all your time.

TWENTY-FIVE

ZERO-DOWN REAL ESTATE INVESTING

AN YOU *buy* REAL ESTATE WITH ZERO DOLLARS down? In 2011, I learned how and never looked back. This is knowledge you may learn in the fancy real estate seminars, though there can be a few small hurdles along the way. There are several scenarios when this may be possible. Here I will focus on a few of my favourites that give you 100% control over the property.

Step one in this process would be to find an undervalued property. You need to be able to secure a property where the price of the property and cost of the renovations do not total more than 80% of the appraised value once it's complete. An undervalued property such as the one I'm describing could be changed by simply adding an income suite, tenant profile, or anything from simple to elaborate renovations.

So, you found an undervalued property. Now what? How do you se-cure it without any money from your pocket? You can do this several ways. Here are a few idea starters:

- Provide/acquire a minimum of 20% down by way of savings, or get a family member, friend, or other joint-venture partner involved. Use it as a down payment for a short-term purchase plus improvements or a mortgage. Once you fix up the property, get an after-completion appraisal and refinance. After the refinance, you will be able to pay back your 20% loan and have 100% control of the property with zero down and a 20% equity position.

- Get unsecured or secured lines of credit and credit cards to come up with an unencumbered down payment or full amount of the property and renovation cost.

- Move into a small multifamily property. This usually requires a small down payment (generally 5%).

- Look to get a purchase plus improvements mortgage. Even better, add a suite to an owner-occupied property, then get a new appraisal and refinance. This might take a construction-type loan, but any experienced mortgage broker can hook you up.

- Use personal savings. Start with an owner-occupied property to build this up. Don't worry—for every dime you put in, you will get that out and more in a short period of time.

- Find a significantly undervalued property and then bring the deal with the renovation plan to a hard-money lender. (Many mortgage brokers have access to folks who can help.) They will have control of the property until it is refinanced.

- Find a great deal and offer up a joint venture partnership to folks who can provide the cash.

This was my path to buying four properties with zero dollars out of pocket. It was 2011, and at this point in my real estate career, I was out of cash. Over the previous two years, I purchased six properties with conventional down payment money and some joint venture money.

I needed to do something different. The real estate industry was still reeling from the effects of the great recession. Interest rates were low, and lending restrictions were high.

I felt stuck, so I turned to one of my property managers for advice. He had a huge multifamily portfolio of his own, and we'd developed a relationship over the years. I met with him one afternoon and asked about his business model. He was taking over run-down or abandoned C-grade apartment buildings. He fixed them up, repositioned them in the marketplace, and refinanced them. Then he'd take all his money out and more and do it again.

I left that meeting wondering if I could apply the same theory to a small property.

That day, I went on a search for an undervalued property that was within my means. I'd accumulated a few unsecured lines of credit while purchasing the other properties, so although my resources were limited, I could deploy just about $100K unsecured. I found a single-family bungalow in poor condition. The less-than-ideal tenants had just left, and though the place was trashed, I thought it was perfect.

Many people say they want to buy undervalued properties, but when they walk in, they get overwhelmed by smells, rodents, and junk, so they walk away. This little house had good bones, and the zoning allowed for four units on the property. I bought it and did a basic renovation. I added new kitchen cabinets and a new bathroom vanity, painted the tub and tub surround, recaulked it, painted the entire property, put down new flooring in the bedrooms and kitchen, cleaned the carpets, cut down a bunch of overgrowth in the yard, changed the light fixtures, and voilà—I was ready for a post-renovation appraisal.

I spoke to a mortgage broker and based a mortgage approval on our assumed appraisal number and moved forward. When an appraiser came out, he gave me a crazy low price. It was incredibly disheartening to learn my first zero-down project was going to be a big fat loss. Fortunately, my mortgage broker and I were able to build a case with comps from the area, as well as pictures and info on the house, and got a second chance with a different appraisal company.

Long story short, after another couple of weeks of sweating it out, we ended up with a cheque from the mortgage company that covered the cost of the house, all the renovations, and an additional $10,000. Not only that, but we also had a house with a 20% equity position and a tenant in place.

I framed a copy of the cheque from the mortgage company and put it on my wall for motivation. Although there were a few tense moments, it felt easy, and was almost too good to be true. Maybe once was just luck. I knew if I ever wanted to write about it, I would have to do it again.

So, Shelly and I tackled project number two. It was a grand old Victorian house we instantly fell in love with. The house was mostly abandoned, except for a squatter and some rats. The yard was full of junk and debris, including old, rusting cars. But it spoke to us. As we walked around this once-grand old house steeped in history, we felt a connection to it. It was used as a hotel in the late 1800s—then as a boardinghouse, a bed-and-breakfast, and later as a half-assed triplex. The paint was faded, a lot of the siding was rotten (in some places you could see right into the house), the windows were awful, the doors were falling off, and it had a second-story deck that appeared ready to fall off the back.

Why would such a property speak to us? We think it had something to do with the trim, the yard, and the amazing rock wall peeking out from the undergrowth in the back that gave it a unique charm. You could almost hear the ship builders who would have stayed there back in the day. As we entered the house, it was still partially furnished from tenants who likely moved out when the heating system stopped working and the pipes froze in several places during the winter months. I can remember a large aquarium full of dirty water and dead fish. One area had a hole in the roof where someone removed the chimney and woodstove below.

What you must understand is that, beneath the dirt and grime, we could see things like amazing tile work, thick baseboards, and a huge kitchen sink. You could see the past pride of ownership and expense in the craftsmanship (which the Victorians were great at). We checked out the electrical system, or what was left of it. Jumper cables—yeah, the ones used for cars—had been used to take power from one unit and provide it to the other. The ductwork from the defunct heating system had holes in it from the rats.

The stench in that area of the house was unbelievable. However, next to the "modern" heating system was an old, abandoned coal-fired furnace. You could almost see a person with a shovel trying to keep this old house warm. We broke a rule that day and brought some family members along to check out the house with us. They did stay quiet most of the time, because they could see the passion in our eyes for this old dump. Even our real estate agent had to bite his tongue. Later, after the finished product was revealed, they all admitted they thought we were crazy to take on such a huge project.

TWENTY-SIX

JOINT VENTURE DEALS

USING *other* PEOPLE'S MONEY IS THE BEST WAY to buy real estate. You may have heard of joint venture deals and wonder if they're just a myth—something that's too good to be true. I mean, can you really buy real estate with somebody else's money? The truth is there are several ways that this can be done if you are flexible on the term "own."

So, what is a joint venture as it relates to buying real estate? In simple terms, it's an agreement between two or more parties to share resources with the intent of purchasing a property.[27] It requires a benefit to both parties. An example would be someone with cash and another person with construction skills. The split could be 50–50, 80–20, or any other variation.

There are many books and videos that may make it sound as if joint venture partnerships are easy to form. That is not true, and it can be a very difficult road. I want to say that up front so that you won't be disappointed when you go out and start facing rejection. Rejection, in this instance, is part of the process.

I used to ask why someone with money would want to give up 50% of a real estate deal to a person with no money. In theory they could just take the money and buy the property themselves. As I have matured in the real estate investing business and have experienced the ups, downs, and many challenges of operating properties, a lightbulb has turned on. I now realize the money person is in an enviable position. They can provide a down payment and renovation costs, then sit back while their partner does all the work.

If the property is a good investment, they get an amazing return on their money and get to own 50% of the property from a passive position. The secret to this of course is to not oversell the passive position as it relates to money. A solid, lawyer-reviewed agreement would be a wise idea in these types of relationships. Many of these arrangements go sideways due to greed, misunderstandings, bad property management, unexpected repairs, and unexpected financial returns.

Let's face it—do you ever actually own 100% of your real estate asset? Even if you pay off your mortgage, you will still have to pay property tax, land lease payments, or condominium fees.

Would you rather "own" zero properties or a piece of several? That is a personal question that every investor will need to answer for themselves. Some of the questions you should ask yourself before considering this type of real estate investing are as follows:

- ⊙ What phase of your life are you in? Do you have children?

- ⊙ What skill sets do you have? What do you have to offer in the deal? This could include land-zoning experience, building supplies, construction or carpentry skills, and access to construction equipment or cash.

- ⊙ Do you know lenders who want to participate in lending to real estate investors?

- ⊙ Do you know any tired landlords looking to unload properties? They might be willing to help with all or part of a mortgage (vendor take back) or set it up like a rent-to-own deal with 100% financing. You'll need to understand the limitations of the area in which you want to invest. Real estate is all about supply and demand. If you're seeking a tired landlord willing to do a partial or 100% deal with you, I would stay away from highly desirable, overheated markets like Manhattan or Vancouver. If you found a property under market value in one of those areas, you could likely find a joint venture partner to help you buy it.

You will have better luck finding zero-down deals in secondary or gentrifying markets. Look for properties in smaller towns and cities.

So, now we know what to look for. How do we find these money partners? When I first started investing, I talked about it with a friend who shared my interest. We decided the best way to get started would be to split the renovation cost and down payment and start buying properties. At the time, we only needed 5% down for two-unit properties and 10% for three to four units. The year was 2009, and we both had great credit. Looking back, I'm not sure if I needed a partner, but it did give me the confidence to move forward.

The challenge was that my partner lived in a different part of the country from where we were investing, so it forced me to do the heavy lifting, organizing, and renovating, as well as managing the properties. It did allow us to easily buy six properties in a very short period.

We still own a few of those properties together, and since they are stable and low maintenance, my wife, Shelly, and I don't mind looking after them. Also, our relationship with our friend is solid, so he takes a chill approach and trusts our judgment when we say something needs to be done. I would caution going into business with friends or family. One of the largest risks is an unavoidable "cash call."

Here's an example. You and your friend or family member come up with a down payment and buy a property 50–50. You own the property for a couple of years, and one day discover a leaky roof. The job costs $10,000, and it's two weeks before Christmas. That means each of you needs to come up with $5,000 immediately. The reality is when you own properties, unexpected repair costs are quite common. If the up-front expectations are not set, it can turn a good partnership bad, really quickly.

Other considerations that will need to be made include things like renovations. Let's say you buy a property in an up-and-coming area. Maybe your basic trim was okay at first, but now your competitors offer en suite laundry and dishwashers in all their units. You have a tenant move out and are now forced to upgrade to the new standard. Are these upgrades necessary? That can often be a judgment call. It'll likely require a cash call, and when you form your partnership, you need to determine who is going to lead these conversations to prevent confusion and frustration when these issues come up.

If you don't have a friend or family member to invest with, how else can you get money? I often think back to my flipping days and realize that the major banks are pretty good partners. They are unemotional, and as soon as they agree to a deal, they stay out of your business if you make the payments.

Of course, there are many challenges to this method, such as credit ratings, unencumbered down payments, maxing out on the amount of mortgages lenders allow, and debt-service ratios. If this causes issues, how are you going to buy properties? If you need inspiration, look to investors or companies that are a few steps ahead of you. Then scale back.

Here are some idea starters that hopefully can help send you on the right path:

- *Find a like-minded friend or family member.* It may only take one loan and a refinance to get you going. Do not over complicate it. Set a goal, plan, and follow the plan.

- *Run an ad looking for distressed properties.* You may find owners of old buildings who are willing to do a vendor take back loan.

- *Join a real estate forum like BiggerPockets, or a local real estate group.* You can also seek out joint venture partners.

- *Talk to mortgage brokers.* Many have connections to people who are interested in investing in real estate but don't have the time or skill to find deals, renovate and manage properties, or organize any of the work that goes into it.

- *Do not underestimate the value of your skills.* Some valuable skills you may have include the following:
  - The ability to find great deals
  - The vision to turn a bad property into a good one (including adding value, like additional units)
  - Knowledge about building codes and city planning, development, and zoning laws
  - Skills like construction, plumbing, carpentry, electrical, project management, landscaping, or painting
  - The equipment to take on repair jobs, such as demoli-

tion tools, dump trailers, and brute strength

- Property management experience

- Business plan creation experience

- Connections with people who can provide more capital to fund more projects

- ⊙ *Join a local real estate group.* Meetup.com is a great place to search for a group. Often potential joint venture partners may show up. When you walk into a room of real estate investors, you're all likely looking for the same thing—to build a property portfolio.

- ⊙ *Meet and get close to people.* Maybe you will find a great partner.

I will caution you that there are many pitfalls to partnerships, and you need to make sure you are compliant with local securities and exchange commission laws, especially if you have less than a million dollars in net worth or make less than $250K per year.

Also keep in mind that the key to any joint venture relationship is to have an exit strategy—not only a simple exit strategy but one based on various circumstances. This includes death, illness, financial hardship, lack of desire to be in the partnership, a predetermined time to list the property for sale, a shotgun close, and a buyout option for each partner.

TWENTY-SEVEN

FLIPPING HOUSES

IT ALL STARTED IN *the* EARLY 2000S. THE first one was a 650-square-foot, one-bedroom condominium with a fantastic view. While the property was dated, it didn't need a ton of work. In my mind, it was a simple project, so my wife, Shelly, and I used a move-in, fix-up, and sell approach. This is a great approach when it comes to maximizing profit, but you need to be willing to live in a construction project most of the time. This was sometimes a challenge when it came to dust, disorganized clothes and furniture, and of course, sometimes-limited use of kitchens and bathrooms. But other than the annoyance factor, this has served us well financially.

Some places sold fast, while others took more time. There was one place we sold and then rented back from the buyers to allow us time to find our next projects. There were other times when we had to move home to my parents' house (which became a challenge once we had our first child). The key here is being flexible with your living situation while you're renovating properties.

One thing to keep in mind is that if you find properties in a quickly appreciating market or right after a low point in the market cycle, you can often make money on flips doing very little. Just buy it, fix up the kitchen and bathroom, and add curb appeal. (Bark mulch, paint, and siding can be great for this.)

Another thing you'll want to try to do is find properties that appeal to a wide audience. This typically means a property with three bedrooms and two bathrooms in an area close to good schools, shopping, roadway infrastructure, public transit routes, and hospitals. In the U.S., look at what military personnel are buying and try to meet the VA loan requirements.

A great strategy is to look for average homes and do many projects rather than look for a luxury single flip that you hope will be hugely profitable. The profit margins in each flip might be less; however, so will your risk and number of projects you will be able to find and do. When you get into large, expensive projects, they often take longer to sell, which can cause the carrying costs to eat up a lot of your profit margin. When you buy a regular house in a regular neighbourhood, it will appeal to more buyers, and often a quick update to kitchens, bathrooms and flooring can make a huge difference to the value.

The idea of flipping houses is often romanticized. Popular TV shows and travelling seminars make it look easy and profitable. You and your wife find an undervalued property, set out a vision, do most of the work yourself, and sell it for a huge profit. But the reality is that while many flips work out, many fail. Common reasons for this can include cost overruns, taking too long to sell, and running out of money before the project is complete.

If you want to flip, step one is to read the room. Know the area, look at comps, and see what is selling, for how much, and why. It's also a good idea to drive by recently purchased homes. What renovations appear to have been done?

You should know, too, that there are often huge opportunities to be found in homes owned by seniors, as they often live in dated houses in amazing neighbourhoods. There's an old joke that the best place to find real estate opportunities is at a funeral. As crass as that may sound, there's a lot of truth to it. Although you may not wish to crash a funeral, you could send letters, drop notes in mailboxes, and contact lawyers who deal with a lot of estates.

The main trait for a successful flipper is vision. You need to be able to see the finished product while standing in a dump. You need to be able to knock down walls and see spaces in three dimensions. But just because you need vision doesn't mean you have to do it all alone.

Once you identify your weaknesses, you need to hire professionals who can fill in the gaps.

I've worked with some interior designers over the years who have opened my eyes to a completely new way of thinking about space. When you're ready to go to market and you decide to buy or lease furniture, have a staging company handle the arrangements. You may sell it furnished, completely turnkey, or decide to rent the furniture instead. The details are what will make the sale of the property fast and easy.

Often what happens is you start with a grand vision, and then as the project comes close to completion, the tendency is to try to cut costs. The problem is that the end is the worst time to cut costs. The plan from the beginning needs to include timeline variances, and a plan B. Many large renovations start with a cut job and end with a teardown to the foundation. (Sometimes it is cheaper to start over.)

To keep things on track, set up checkpoints and consider hiring a project manager to keep all the tradespeople on track and in order. It can also be a good idea to offer early completion bonuses to your team and figure out the carrying costs. Sometimes it's cheaper to hire more people and get the project to market. I've painfully watched and consulted with do-it-yourself, weekend warrior–type folks who lose most or all of their profit when they take too long to finish a project. Carrying costs include things like mortgage payments, property taxes, utilities, insurance, lawn care, snow removal, and port-a-potty rentals.

PRIVATE SALES AND FORECLOSURES

PRIVATE-SALE PROPERTIES *are* **A GREAT WAY TO GET** a good deal. I've purchased two properties that were private-sale listings. I have also been offered countless other opportunities but have referred many of them to other investors I know.

Each situation was different, and each offered a win-win solution.

So, how do you find them? I placed an ad on Kijiji and searched for properties in poor condition. I received a response from a person with a triplex they were tired of owning in an area I was interested in. It was in rough condition and had a vacant unit and two other units that had undesirable tenants occupying the units.

I walked through the property with the current owner and my property manager, with the latter being the person who would eventually manage the property. We negotiated a cash offer with a quick closing. I made a deal with the existing tenants to move out if I agreed to pay them a lump sum in cash. The condition of the property would not permit me to renovate with tenants living in the units.

Some of the renovations included new bathrooms and a new electrical panel along with most of the wiring, insulation, and almost all the windows and doors. We also converted the property to electric heat and got rid of the oil furnace. After it was complete, I was able to get it appraised, refinance it, and find some great tenants—all while getting 100% of my money back.

You might ask why a person wouldn't just fix up their property and sell it for more. The problem is many landlords get tired of being a landlord, especially if they only have one or two units and a busy life. In this case the owners had other business interests that appeared to be quite lucrative, and this triplex was a thorn in their side. It was a relief for them to be able to cut it loose, even at a reduced rate.

You can also place a want ad on a site like Craigslist. I've made two private-sale purchases this way and have reviewed others. I placed a free ad for exactly what I was looking for and waited. I also set alerts for exactly what I was looking for. This has allowed me to find deals in areas I was not interested in and pass the information off to other investors who were more than happy to pay for the lead if they reached a deal with the seller. In fact, some people use wholesaling as a strategy for investing in real estate. Find the deal, secure it, and have a provision to transfer it at a markup. As an alternative, you can ask for a set referral fee for each deal you pass off that results in a final agreement.

No matter what the economic conditions are or the area you're looking in, there will always be foreclosures available. The downside is that many times when a property is going into foreclosure, the owner has other financial problems and has borrowed the maximum amount against the property. This can mean a house will be way underwater by the time it reaches a foreclosure sale.

The truth is that lending institutions want to lend money and collect payments. They don't want to be in the property ownership and management business because they're in the lending business. Lenders would prefer that payments are made on time. Before a property reaches the foreclosure process, the lender will usually try to work out a deal to get payments caught up. That could mean anything from forgiving a payment to adding time to the term of the loan.

When all options are exhausted, the primary lender will start the foreclosure process.

There are many reasons properties fall into this category, and they are often great opportunities.

Some of the reasons homes are foreclosed include the following situations:

- Tax liens

- Judgements

- Code violations

- Divorce

- Negative equity

- Vacant and cannot sell

- Flips gone wrong

- Inheritance

- Probate

- ⊙ Trustees

- ⊙ Cash buyers

- ⊙ Bankruptcies

- ⊙ HOA liens

- ⊙ Bylaw or zoning violations and permit violations

- ⊙ Environmental problems

- ⊙ Bad evictions that have significantly damaged the property

- ⊙ Tax issues

- ⊙ Pre-foreclosures

- ⊙ Other financial issues

One reason I wanted to find foreclosure listings is because I enjoy the thrill of the hunt. When I started looking for real estate opportunities, I would drive around areas I was interested in. I started to notice some properties that looked vacant and often had a couple of papers stuck to the windows. Generally, it was two sheets that were 8.5 by 11 inches. I was a bit shy and nervous at first and was afraid to go and check them out. When I finally got the nerve and walked up to the properties, I felt like I'd found gold.

One of the sheets was from a property management company stating that the property had been secured and was being watched, so stay away. The other sheet had legal and bank information about the foreclosure. I found out that when this notification was posted, it could be several months before the property made its way through the court process.

I contacted the lawyers involved to see if I could buy the property before it went through the full foreclosure process. This form of communication was met with mixed results. Some of the contacts were helpful and provided an update as to when the property might be going up for auction. Others I spoke with made me feel as if I was bugging them, and they wanted to get off the phone.

What I did learn was that if I kept track of the property, it would eventually show up in the local court or be listed by a real estate agent. That's when I had the real estate agent I was dealing with alert me of any bank-owned properties hitting the market. I also went to the local courthouse to find out which properties were in the process of foreclosure.

The challenge with many of the properties that are in foreclosure is that the amount owed is much higher than the value. In many cases the owner has refinanced and pushed the amount they could borrow against the property to the edge. That is generally when payments are missed and the property enters the foreclosure process.

In areas that have an abundance of foreclosures, you will often find foreclosure auctions. In smaller areas you may find that only a handful of lawyers or real estate agents deal with foreclosure properties. There are many ways to tap into the foreclosure-property scene, and it often depends on the area in which you are located.

You also do not want to forget the old-school way. In the case of Halifax, Nova Scotia, foreclosure listings are located at the Provincial Supreme Court on Lower Water Street.

The first time I headed to the courthouse to check it out, I was a bit nervous. I had no idea where exactly I was going, who to ask, or what exactly I was asking for. When I walked into the courthouse, I was a bit intimidated. However, the guard at the front desk was friendly and directed me to an office.

When I entered the office, there were several clerks behind glass. They seemed to all put their heads down when I walked over, but I managed to get one of them to look up and point to a bulletin board with the information I was looking for. The mystery was solved. It turned out to be easier than expected.

I copied down the information. If you pay, they do allow you to photocopy the listings, or you can take a picture with your phone. What the listings offer is a court date that tells you when the properties are going up for auction, the names of the owners, the lender, and in most cases, the balance owed.

It's important to note that just because a property is in the foreclosure process, it may not make it to the auction block (if a deal is reached with the lender). In some instances, the bank will not want to let it go for super cheap. If you do go to a foreclosure auction, you will need to have money set up and ready to go. In Halifax you are required to pay 10% immediately after winning a bid, and you have 10 days to provide the balance.

Since so many people ask me about finding listings, I figured, Why not post them monthly on my blog? I had only made a few posts and was reached out to by an acquaintance. This individual was also a financial backer of a local businessperson who was in financial trouble. He asked me to remove the information about his pending foreclosure because he did not want anyone to know how bad the financial position of this person was. I did remove it, but it made me realize that often we are clouded by the opportunity to get a great real estate deal and forget about the personal circumstances behind the financial situation that led to the great deal.

This thought pattern has led me to discover better ways to negotiate deals so that it's a win-win for the seller and buyer. For example, a friend of mine purchased a house from a homeowner who was facing a business bankruptcy. He was able to purchase the home and rent it back to the owner while they finalized a divorce and sorted out their finances. It allowed them to stay in their home and put cash in their pocket. It was a real win-win for both parties. You can even provide a first right of refusal to the tenant (former owner) should you ever want to sell so they can be in a good position to buy it back from you.

You can also turn these kinds of situations into a rent-to-own scenario. I admire countries like the U.S. that have more ways to solve seller problems. Short sales are one example that allow a buyer to buy a home for less than is owed on it in order to avoid it entering the often lengthy and expensive foreclosure process.

TWENTY-NINE

TAX SALE

A **TAX SALE IS A** *town* **OR CITY'S LAST** resort to collect owed property tax and turn the property over to a property owner who will pay the tax. The city or town will make numerous attempts to collect the money from the property owner before the property is auctioned off.

I've heard hero stories about people making huge profits buying and flipping tax sale properties. I wanted to find out what it was all about, so I figured I'd gain experience by attending a small-town tax sale.

Shelly and I own properties in her hometown (Digby, Nova Scotia). I figured this would be a good place to start. I googled "tax sale Digby," and in the search results, I found information on the municipality of Digby's upcoming tax sale. There was a list of all the properties and owners' names on the municipality website.

I searched for properties that I found interesting, then had our area property manager drive by and take pictures. You can't enter the properties, but you can view them from the outside. A lot of the properties listed were land only. There were a few on my list with houses, but the homes were in rough condition.

In the case of the sale I attended, the properties (approximately 30) were a minimum of three years in arrears. This means the owners of these properties hadn't paid tax for a minimum of three years.

If you were the successful bidder on a property, the property owner had six months after the sale to pay the taxes and redeem the property. Which meant If you were the high bidder and paid for the property, you had to wait six months before you had access it.

When I arrived at the sale, the parking lot was packed. I walked into the building, and it was clear that everyone was there for the sale. I was given a list of the properties that were going to be auctioned off. The amount of tax and fees owed was also listed. That portion of the bid was required to be paid immediately. The balance had to be paid in three business days.

I walked into the council chambers where the auction was being held. I managed to find a chair and waited for the bidding to start. The auctioneer went over the rules, and then the bidding began. What you were instructed to do to place a bid was to state your name and amount of the bid. The bidding starts at the amount of tax and fees owed, which on some of these rural lots was as low as $400. This of course was a starting bid, so some waterfront properties reached $60,000. The taxes owed and any fees associated with the property were to be paid on the spot with either credit card, certified cheques, debit, or bank draft. (You have three days to pay the balance.)

I almost made a mistake and got caught up in the action. I wanted to buy something, and since all the properties on my list got redeemed before the sale, I re-evaluated the list. A property with a dwelling was coming up, and the starting bid was $2,539. I figured, How bad could it be? A house that I could rent for $2,539 would be a steal. I tried to view it on Google Earth, but it was on a back road, and a blurry picture was the best I could get. There was only one bidder on the property, and as they were about to do the final call for bids, my rational side kicked in, and I resisted the temptation to bid. The successful bidder got it for the taxes owing $2,539.

I picked up Shelly after the sale and told her we were going to drive by a house. I was going to either say, "Thank God I did not buy that," or "Damn, I missed a great deal." We drove by the house, and I am glad I did not get it. It was a dump on a small lot and was surrounded by other abandoned houses. I would base the real estate value at very close to zero. I'm not sure what happened to the owner, but clearly no one had been living in the house for a long time.

I would describe the people who attended the event as coming from all walks of life. Some were older people, some younger people, and many were from all over the province. One thing that everyone had in common was they were hoping for a great deal on a piece of real estate. There was a great, optimistic energy in the room. I'm sure some people went away happy, while others who were caught up in bidding wars were not too happy. I saw some people who were extremely frustrated. There were some folks who did not bid on anything, and others who bid on everything.

While I didn't get anything the first go-round, I'm excited to attend another tax sale. I do realize that you may have to look and bid on several properties before you get a great deal and will need to do your research and only bid on what you plan to buy.

Here is a summary of how it all works:

1. *Find a tax sale*: Google "tax sale" and whatever city or town you want to buy real estate in. If they don't have a tax sale listed, send them an email from the "contact us" section of the website.

2. *Check out the listings*: Look at the tax sale listings. Do a drive by, or have someone you can trust do a drive by of the properties and take some pictures.

3. *Decide how much you are willing to pay*: Decide what you are going to bid on and how much you are willing to pay. Don't get carried away and pay too much. Do not let your ego do the bidding for you.

4. *Realize you will now have to pay all future property tax*: Make sure you realize that if you do get the property, you will need to pay the taxes each year. I mention that because some people might be tempted to buy a bunch of cheap parcels of land and then have to pay a bunch of property taxes every year on land they don't necessarily want.

5. *Have cash or a credit card ready on sale day*: You need to pay the tax balance and fees owed at the sale with cash, credit card, bank draft, or certified cheque on the spot. You go from the bidding room right to the cashier. Everything above the taxes and fees owed needs to be paid within three days. You need to have a high-limit credit card ready on sale day and then access to the rest of the cash you will need within three business days of the sale.

6. *If you are the high bidder, you can't move in immediately*: When you are the successful bidder and you pay the fees, your money gets held for six months. The owner has six months to pay the taxes owed and redeem the property. If the property is

redeemed, your cash will be returned to you with interest.

It's also important to realize that every municipality, state, parish, region, or area will likely hold a tax sale at least once per year. Depending on where you are, they set their own rules around property tax collection and disposal of properties that have unpaid taxes owed on them.

There was a tax sale this past week in my home city, so the experience is fresh. Here are 10 tips from the experience that I would recommend that will help to give you the upper hand when buying tax sale properties:

1. Print off a list of the properties that will be offered at the tax sale from your area's website well in advance. Make note of any changes.

2. Locate the properties you're interested in buying and drive to the sites.

3. Understand what "as is" means in your area as related to properties sold by way of a tax sale. When you arrive at the site, cautiously look around. Smell the air close to the building. If you smell oil, mould, gas, etc., you might want to walk away. View the overall condition. Is the property occupied? Is it in an area you want to own a property in? What is your first impression, and can you achieve what you want based on the appearance? In my area, the city takes zero responsibility for any environmental, physical, or occupant issues with properties sold at a tax sale.

4. Determine the maximum price you will pay for the properties you selected, and make sure they'll meet your investment criteria for the purchase. Is it a flip as is, a flip renovated, a buy and hold with a current building, or a teardown vacant land hold? If the property is vacant, can you get it rezoned? Or is it worth holding as vacant land?

5. Make sure you are aware of the accepted forms of payment at the tax sale you plan to attend.

6. Keep your emotions in check. It's a good idea to bring a bank draft made out to the city for the required starting bid of the property or properties you have selected. If you don't buy them, you can take the cheque back to the bank. When you're bidding, don't let emotion take over. The reason it is an auction is to make it fair and competitive. Keep your emotions in check. If you don't get a property, that's ok. It's better to miss out on a property than to pay too much.

7. Understand the redemption period (if one exists). In the sale I attended this past week, there were 17 redeemable and one nonredeemable properties. What this means is that even if you had a high bid and purchased a property, if it was labelled redeemable, the deeded owner only has six months to pay the tax bill, interest on your money, cost of insurance, and any additional costs to secure the building during the redemption period (boarding up windows, patching the roof, mowing the lawn, etc.). If the property is nonredeemable, then you get to take full ownership right away. It also means it has likely been vacant for a long period of time.

8. Understand the rules around current occupants in the property. When you buy a tax sale property, they're sold truly as is. That means they could be occupied by tenants who are willing to pay rent, tenants who are unwilling to pay rent, a family member of the deeded owner who cannot pay to purchase the property but has been living in it for several years (possibly with mental or physical limitations). It could be occupied by squatters (people who just decided to move in); it could be occupied by drug users, drug dealers, or prostitutes. It could have rodents or other animals living in it too. In the case of

the tax sale I attended, it's up to the buyer to work with the local residential tenancy board, police, pest control, and animal control to deal with current occupants. The good news is that you can start working on your evictions or new lease arrangements right away. You'll have six months to clean up the occupant issues.

9. Plan accordingly when you purchase a tax sale property. You may think you know what you want to do with it before the sale. The plan may change based on the true condition of the property once you own it. It may change from a buy and hold to a complete teardown. You may discover that it's a poor fit for your investment portfolio and decide to sell it. You may decide to flip it as is. Whatever you decide to do, you'll likely have a redemption period to plan and decide which direction your project is going to go in.

10. Understand your personal risk tolerance. When you buy a property from a tax sale, it's a risky investment. Like most high-risk investments, if they work out, they have high returns. If they do not work out, it's almost always a negative result. Make sure you think about the emotional impact of paying thousands of dollars for a property that you cannot properly inspect before you purchase. When you buy from a tax sale, it's a gamble.

RENT TO OWN

THE HOUSING *market* APPEARED TO BE AT AN all-time high. We had one single-family home in our portfolio with a long-term tenant. It didn't fit with our portfolio, and prior to the existing tenants, we'd had a series of some not-so-great tenants. One of them had even turned part of the property into a grow-op (they were growing marijuana). When our property manager mentioned it could be a good time to sell, we agreed, and he went on to share the news with the tenants.

The tenants had lived in the home for three years. They were low maintenance and had just recently started a family. They also had family in the area, so the location suited them. When my property manager first met with them, they said no problem and understood that a new buyer may want to occupy the home or change the rent if they were going to keep it as an investment property.

We started planning for the listing, but then about a week later, the tenants called to see if they could buy the house. They were not sure if they could but wanted to try. Due to their credit situation and declared income, a conventional mortgage would have been a challenge. While I knew I shouldn't mix emotion with business, this young family made me ask my property manager to explore some options.

I wanted to sell, take the cash, and reinvest it, so I needed a clean break. This is where a rent-to-own investor who my property manager knew came into the picture. The rent-to-own investor met with the tenants and told them what would be required to move forward. Here are the basics of how things went down, with the tenant agreeing to the following conditions:

- Pay for the legal work required (rent-to-own agreement, closing costs).

- Pay a down payment.

- Agree to a price that would allow them to complete the transaction in three years. Basically, a postdated purchase and sale agreement.

- Agree to pay a higher-than-market rent in those three years. A portion of the rent amount would be credited back to them to use as a down payment on the home.

- Agree to look after maintenance and repairs on the home unless the costs exceeded $500. In this case the cost would be split between the landlord and tenant buyer.

The deal went together smooth as silk, and I believe it is a win-win for me, the tenant (buyers), and the rent-to-own investor.

Rent-to-own is an option that involves the seller making an agreement with a buyer to purchase a property. The buyer in this case doesn't have a large enough down payment or the ability to get a conventional mortgage. The buyer will then pay above-average rent, and a portion of the monthly rent payment will go toward a down payment to purchase the home at a future date. The term might vary in order to meet a set dollar amount or a specific year.

These deals favour the seller by offering a premium on monthly rental revenue and a higher-than-market price for the property at the end of the term. In most cases it would involve a seller, a tenant/buyer, and a rent-to-own investor.

I've read about other rent-to-own scenarios, such as just taking payments on a property until it is paid off without a proper mortgage document. Another scenario might be a landlord charging above average rent with a promise that's not necessarily fully documented to sell the house at a future date. The landlord in this case may say they're saving rent credits equivalent to a portion of the rent. I don't have any firsthand experience with these types of scenarios but felt I should mention them to provide a full understanding of the possibilities.

In this type of agreement, what's important is that you weigh the pros and cons and decide what you want out of the deal. Factors such as time of deal completion, exit strategy if the person cannot get approved, and repercussions if the obligations of the agreement are not met should all be considered. Let's take a closer look at the pros and cons of rent-to-own agreements.

PROS

- You get to help someone purchase a house or property that they may not have been able to purchase otherwise.

- You can sell a property that might be tough to profit from.

- ⊙ There's an opportunity to get a premium price for a property with a predetermined closing date.

- ⊙ The amount of monthly rent will usually be above market rates. (Some owners will charge above market rent and build a rent credit account that can be used toward the down payment. For example, the market rent is $1,000 and the actual rent is $1,300, so $300 would be set aside and given back to the tenant buyer upon completion of the deal.)

- ⊙ You can get a cash down payment up front in the form of a nonrefundable deposit.

- ⊙ A steady stream of monthly income will be possible without having to take care of tenant complaints, property management, or the cost of maintenance and repairs.

- ⊙ If you have a proven track record, it may be easier to find joint venture partners who would be willing to invest money into your portfolio.

- ⊙ If the tenant/buyer backs out of the deal, you get to keep the down payment money and any rent credits, and you still have control of the property to find another buyer or sell the property.

- ⊙ If you have a good rent-to-own client, it could mean a trouble-free experience for you. Think about a property without any calls in the middle of the night about a plumbing or heating issue.

This might seem like the perfect scenario and like everyone should do it. So why don't they?

CONS

- ⊙ Finding a property that will work for your rent-to-own client can be difficult. If the market is appreciating quickly, this might not be a problem. However, don't forget that your exit strategy depends on your tenant/buyer being able to get a mortgage from a conventional lender in a 24- to 36-month period. That will most likely require an appraisal.

- ⊙ Even if you agree to a selling price with your tenant/buyer, it needs to make sense.

- ⊙ Finding a qualified tenant/buyer can be difficult. Often the people looking for rent-to-own deals may not have good credit, a solid employment status, or the ability to put any money down.

- ⊙ Even if they agree to your terms, you will need to have some qualifying criteria to protect yourself.

- ⊙ When things go wrong, you are the bad guy.

- ⊙ Ask yourself what happens in the following circumstances:
  - A couple breaks up.
  - The renter needs to move away for their job and can't complete the contract.
  - The renter loses their job and can't pay rent.
  - The property requires a major repair, like a roof or heating system.

Keep in mind that when things go wrong in people's lives, they often will try to pass the responsibility onto others. If you decide to do rent-to-own agreements, you will need to use a lawyer to represent you and require your tenant buyers to use a lawyer so they have a full understanding of the agreement and what happens in circumstances like the ones listed.

Here's why. Let's say your tenant/buyer loses his job, and the only other job he can get is in another city. So he calls you to cancel the contract and get some or all his down payment money back to move with. You refer him to the agreement, and voilà, you're the bad guy.

Or perhaps you arranged for a rent-to-own buyer to take over some old properties you own. The investor puts a bunch of work into the properties. However, based on conditions, local markets, or tenant profiles, they cannot afford the payments. So you take back your renovated properties, keep any down payment money, and become the bad guy.

On the other hand, if you're an investor who would like to acquire properties but have limited resources, a rent-to-own situation could be perfect for you. You might be able to help a landlord get a steady stream of income and take the property management burden off their shoulders at the same time, building up equity. This would be a good situation for a hands-on type of investor who can do their own maintenance and repairs as well as property management. This could also be a way to buy multiple properties. The areas to look for these opportunities would be in secondary markets.

Other pros for a tenant buyer would be perhaps a tenant who's on the path to rebuilding their credit and cannot get a mortgage from a traditional lender. They might have enough cash for a down payment but still don't qualify. This can get them on the path to home ownership. People like the idea of owning their home, so this capitalizes on that notion. There are some great books and experts in this field who can help if it is the right opportunity for you. I have a realtor friend with a lot of experiences setting up these kinds of transactions.

Having worked with several real estate investors in Nova Scotia who set up these kinds of deals, I've collected some of the advice they offered about rent-to-own opportunities:

- ⊙ Get an agreement of purchase and sale at a further date (two to three years). This should include a nonrefundable 5% deposit (for if the buyer backs out) and other clauses for protection.

- ⊙ Get a tenancy lease that's between the tenant and rent-to-own buyer and you as the investor and landlord.

I personally find that most real estate professionals have little experience with rent-to-own transactions, including lawyers. This is despite the fact that it seems to be a very popular option in major provinces like Ontario, Quebec, and British Columbia.[28] It can also be a hard concept to explain to potential rent-to-own buyers since many have been conventional renters and do not understand all the costs that go into purchasing a property such as legal work, inspections, appraisals, maintenance, deed-transfer taxes, and insurance. On the other hand, it can be a great strategy to build wealth and help people enter a housing market that they may never get into without someone willing to work with them on a rent-to-own basis.

THIRTY-ONE

CONDOMINIUM INVESTING

WHILE THIS *might* SOUND STRANGE, THERE WAS A time when a condominium (condo) flip ended up with my wife and me in a courtroom.

This happened over a decade ago, before we got into buy and hold real estate investing.

The condo was an '80s two bedroom that was in excellent condition but very dated. Our plan was to modernize it and sell it. We looked at the reserve fund study and noticed a couple of flaws, like an upcoming window replacement project that appeared to be underfunded. We figured this would be no big deal. A $5,000 special assessment would likely handle any shortfalls.

The condo was in a nice area, and many of the unit owners were retired professionals. We also knew that any newer, younger owners could get the amount added on to their mortgage. (Most lenders are pretty cooperative around special assessments.) The condo corporation was also managed by a well-known, large property management company, so we figured it would be all good.

We purchased the condo, submitted our renovation plan to the board, had it approved, and got to work. I went to the annual general meeting shortly after the purchase and got on the board. I will note that most owners don't want to volunteer for the board, so it's easy to get elected.

In my opinion, all unit owners should serve time on the board of directors. It's a thankless job, and you're forced to hear all the complaints from unit owners about everything from a noisy dog to the grass not being cut to the right length. Most condo boards hire an outside property management company, so you end up working closely with them. If you're a property manager of a condo corporation, your role is more of a mediator between the unit owners, board of directors, and vendors doing the work to keep the common areas maintained.

When I joined this particular board, I quickly realized they were in a time of turmoil. Most of the current board members were on the board for a long time and tried to keep condo fees low and avoid any special assessments. They seemed to be unaware of the pending financial problems and were defensive when I asked about some of the upcoming projects that were clearly underfunded. Shortly after I joined the board, a couple of the long-term members quit. We ended up with a small board and our property manager.

When issues arose, we decided to bring them to the attention of the unit owners on a one-on-one basis. I figured the action needed would be obvious. We would go over the reserve fund study, talk about the possible options, hold a general meeting, and then get everyone to agree to a special assessment.

Unfortunately, my vision of what would happen and what actually did happen were completely different. When we met with the individual owners, they seemed to understand what needed to be done. However, some of the old board members formed an unauthorized committee to contradict everything we were saying. We miscalculated the human factor in this business deal.

The new, unauthorized board appeared to have an intent to defend the point of view that we would not need a special assessment or increased condo fees to deal with the problem. I was on the board with two other long-term owners who were feeling betrayed, so we decided to have a meeting with our property manager to discuss options. We decided it was counterproductive to go against the past board members. This was due to the legislation in place that would force our condo corporation to have a reserve fund study completed within the next year.

We all resigned from the board of directors, and my wife and I sold the condo. After we left, a new board was elected, and they ordered a reserve fund study. The reserve fund study led to a special assessment of about $5,000. Although a year had passed, the new owner of our condo accused us of knowing about the special assessment ahead of time. Despite the fact that it would have been impossible for us (or anyone) to predict the future of the board, she took us to court and we settled by paying $5000. This situation was also an important part of my growth as a businessman.

Overall, the concept of condominium ownership is relatively simple and has been around for a long time. Technically, a condominium is a collection of individual home units and common areas along with the land upon which they sit. Individual home ownership within a condominium is construed as ownership of only the airspace confining the boundaries of the home (in Anglo-Saxon law systems; there are different definitions elsewhere). The boundaries of that space are specified by a legal document known as a declaration, filed on record with the local governing authority. Typically these boundaries will include the wall surrounding a condo, allowing the homeowner to make some interior modifications without affecting the common area. Anything outside this boundary is held in an undivided ownership interest by a corporation established at the time of the condominium's creation. The corporation holds this property in trust on behalf of the homeowners as a group—it may not have ownership itself.

Condominiums have conditions, covenants, restrictions, and often additional rules that govern how the individual unit owners are to share the space. It's also possible for a condominium to consist of single-family dwellings. These are called "detached condominiums," and homeowners don't maintain the exteriors of the dwellings or yards. There are also "site condominiums," and these allow the owner to have more control and possible ownership (as in "whole lot" or "lot line" condominiums) over the exterior appearance. These structures are preferred by some planned neighborhoods and gated communities.

The time I've served on condo corporation boards has allowed me to learn a lot about how condo corporations work. As a unit owner, it's important to understand the condo laws for the area they are in as well as the bylaws for the specific condo corporation.

The most important document you need to understand before you buy a condo is called the reserve fund study. In my home province of Nova Scotia, we are quite fortunate. Since 2002, every condo corporation needs an updated reserve fund study to be signed off on by an engineer. It's a requirement of the province of Nova Scotia to have the study updated every five years.

The reserve fund study is basically a guide to the usable life of every major component of the building and the amount of money that's being saved to allow for the cost to fix the problem. For example, if you're looking at a condo in a building and you notice the shingles are old and worn out on the roof, you can check out the section on roof replacement in the reserve fund. If it states the roof needs to be replaced within the next year and they only have $10,000 saved for a $50,000 roof, you need to realize that there are two main ways that a condo corporation will fund a project if they do not have cash. One is to raise condo fees, and the other is to do a special assessment. There are pros and cons to each.

The unfortunate part of condos in our area is that several condo corporations were formed before 2002, and the unit owners, in an effort to keep condo fees low, didn't put enough money aside to replace things like windows, doors, siding, roofs, parking lots, etc. Now many new unit owners are paying large condo fees and special assessments to replace these items.

Here's a breakdown of what I learned:

- ⊙ *Don't forget to calculate the human ego factor.* When I look back, I can see how I clearly stepped on toes and didn't consider the feelings of the past board members. They volunteered countless hours of time trying to do the right thing and felt they were working in the best interests of the unit owners. The unfortunate part of condo boards is that they're made up of owners who quite often have very little business or property management experience. If I could go back in time, I would have consulted with the past board members and got them involved to resolve the problems. At the time, I was younger and more stubborn. I saw a problem with an easy fix and just flexed my ego and went after the solution.

- ⊙ *It's easy to have a renter's mentality.* This is a common problem in most condo corporations. Many people will buy a condo and don't realize that they're buying part of a building. They don't understand that making sure the common areas and things like the roof, windows, siding, doors, hallway, carpets, etc. are all part of the ownership experience. When we were meeting people to gain support for a special assessment, many people didn't feel it was their problem. They felt it should be taken care of by the board. Some people had never attended an AGM (Annual General Meeting) or volunteered any time. It's a challenge to get money for capital projects from people who don't feel they should have to pay. We ran into many people who figured that if the condo fees didn't cover all the costs, then a magic fairy should come and pay. They had no idea that they were part owners of a giant building and that they needed to protect and maintain their own investment.

⊙ *Don't assume that the property manager will make decisions in the best interests of the owners.* When a condo corporation hires a property manager, they're a customer. The property management company wants to keep the board happy. They take on a more neutral role. The job of the property management company is to make sure all financial reports are accurate and provided. They also arrange any work and manage contractors and vendors. They supervise the daily operations of the building. The condo property manager will also help solve disputes between owners and act as a mediator between the unit owners, board of directors, and vendors.

⊙ *Make sure to question the reserve fund study before you buy.* If you're reviewing a reserve fund study before you purchase a condo, make sure to question any problems. Make sure the current board has an answer for any areas that appear to be underfunded. A well-run board will be more than happy to answer any questions from potential buyers.

⊙ *Buyers should beware.* I will have to admit that after this project was completed and we were lucky to have only lost a few thousand dollars, we became a lot more cautious. If you decide to buy a condo, no matter how big or small the building is, make sure to get a good understanding of the maintenance record and future capital expense plan. Now that we own several buildings, we realize it takes a lot of cash to keep them operating properly. Make sure to talk to the current board members and, if possible, current unit owners.

THIRTY-TWO

RAW LAND

A FEW YEARS *back*, THE REDEMPTION PERIOD ended for a tax sale property I purchased. It was a run-down house on a great piece of property I decided to put it up for sale. Little did I know I was about to receive a lesson in raw-land real estate investing. Here is how it played out.

The property had a shabby three-bedroom house on a 10,200-square-foot lot that was zoned for up to four units. I got a great deal on it, and after careful consideration, I decided to sell it as is. I advertised it as a development opportunity since the location was in an up-and-coming area with, of course, the four-unit opportunity.

I ended up selling to a developer, but prior to that, I had some folks ask about the potential of a joint venture partnership, and with that came an education. You see, I thought four units made it valuable, while one potential joint venture partner was thinking that, with the right proposal, we could get an approval for 10 units that we would never build but sell it as an approved deal.

This person was an architect who did a lot of work for some well-known developers and was familiar with how to submit zoning permits to change the land usage. He figured if we could get it zoned for 10 units and provide plans for the 10 units on the property, we could sell it for quite a lot of money. The reason was that it could take two years to bring it to that stage. He explained how builders just want to build, so in turn, a builder could take the plans, sell it as a turnkey investment, and build it right away.

In the end, I just took the quick-cash route. However, it did really open my mind to what raw-land development was all about. Land will always be a good investment. As the saying goes, they aren't making any more of it. If you own land, it provides you with many options.

Though land investing is a great real estate strategy, it does take some of the following considerations:

- A long-term vision

- Up-front capital that may be frozen for several years or decades

- The ability to pay property taxes on land you are holding

- Knowledge of the area and any upcoming changes

- Knowledge of how to apply to the local government for land use or zoning changes

- Knowledge of how to make money off the land while you are holding it for development, including cutting trees on it, mining various stones or soil from it (clay, granite, shale, etc.), bush hogging it for hay, or leasing it for agricultural purposes to farmers

The holder of land has a lot of great partnership options that could allow minimal future investment with huge return on investment. Sometimes this can be strategic, sometimes it's luck.

An example of luck would be in cases where a government agency needs a portion or all your land to build a roadway. Generally, you will get fair market value, and if this is on the back side of a field you're not using, you can benefit without much effort. Strategic investing would be more like accumulating land for cheap prices in an area that will likely become populated in the future.

As with buildings, land values are very location dependent. But that doesn't mean they necessarily need to be in urban locations—just in areas people want to congregate or get away from it all.

Ski hills and amusement parks are a couple of examples of knowing in advance of them being built that it would be a great place to own land. I know of an area near me where an old ski resort is being revitalized. It will require additional accommodations around it if it goes according to plan, and this could provide a great opportunity for a local landowner to build some ski chalets or small hotel.

A ski hill that's 45 minutes from my house has land at the entrance, and the couple who owns the land just had it rezoned to allow them to build some ski chalets and have a common area with a general store. We're looking forward to it being built, as it will provide a great winter getaway for the area—especially since the small town nearby has very limited hotel rooms. The ski season is short where I live (January and February), so the ski hill has also invested in an on-tree climbing maze as well as a host of mountain bike and hiking trails that will make it a year-round destination.

In less rural areas, many landowners have done well buying land just outside of big cities. We have an area that is about a 40-minute drive from the closest downtown core, and it's booming—in fact, almost at an alarming rate. The houses are cheaper, and you can get more for your dollar. With more people than ever working from home, it's an attractive option even for folks working for big companies.

Urban areas are great as well. Many big cities have rougher areas that will eventually be developed. If you can start accumulating land in these areas, they can be great buy and hold investments.

A few years ago, a chat about real estate with a friend of mine led to his personal story about a land lease. He, along with his father, sold their business that was located on land in a busy commercial area. It was an old car dealership that had moved to a new location, so they tore down the building, and the land was vacant.

Then one day they were approached by a major sporting goods retailer to purchase the land. The land was a big portion of my friend's father's retirement plan, so instead of selling it, they worked out a 20-year lease deal with a guaranteed buyout at the end of 20 years. This is currently providing a steady stream of income and includes a great payout at the end.

There are so many religious organizations that have churches and parsonages on valuable sections of land in major cities all over the Western world. In many cases, they can break off portions of their land to allow developers to put up commercial or residential apartment buildings. These land leases are generally set up in 75-year terms.

Without getting into the complicated world of building depreciation, I will use a simple explanation. Buildings have a usable life. When you lease a piece of land, you can put a building on it with an amortization and depreciation schedule. You see, land increases in value, while the building will depreciate. You don't have to pay tax on depreciation, so these land-lease deals are really great financially for developers. There's no up-front expense for land, and they can expense the cost of the lease.

It's also possible to put a defined time on the life of the building and benefit from depreciating it over time. The benefit for the landowner is that they never have to sell the land. They can factor estimated inflation into the lease payment equation (increasing payments over time). The lease may even be renewed or sold at a defined price set out in the beginning.

THIRTY-THREE

OTHER REAL ESTATE INVESTING IDEAS

ABOUT 10 YEARS *ago*, I LOOKED AT A bungalow as a potential investment. It had a main floor unit, a bachelor unit in the basement, and five storage lockers made of plywood and chicken wire that brought in as much revenue as the bachelor apartment without having to deal with a regular tenant.

The self-storage business has been and will continue to grow in the coming years. It can be as simple or as elaborate as you want it to be. Almost any available space in a building or on a piece of land can be storage for somebody.

Years ago, I was hooked on *Storage Wars* and similar shows on Netflix. I mean, they could have done without some of the drama, but I suppose the show would've been dull for many without it. Anyway, it really opened my eyes to the huge variety of things people put in self-storage. Everything from garbage (literal bags of garbage) to vehicles and priceless antiques.

Then I think of every city in Canada and the U.S., and it seems to be a time when older folks are selling their homes and moving into luxury apartments. Most of these apartments are nicer than the homes they're selling. Decisions then have to be made, and what it seems to come down to is either jamming the new luxury apartment with old furniture and belongings or getting a storage locker.

This is despite the fact that if you weighed the cost of a few years' storage with the value of the goods being stored, it would not be worth it. In most cases, it's an emotional decision and not a smart financial decision. It's like my attic in my home. When we moved in, we were down to some final boxes, but rather than go through them, we opted to put them in the attic. I'm sure they will remain there for as long as we live in this house.

When you look at a property, look for storage opportunities. A detached garage can be a great example. You can rent those pretty easily to people who want to store a vehicle or to contractors who need space for tools and supplies. Don't automatically include it with the main property. It could be a dry basement or even something like used shipping containers that can be a great revenue earner. My friend rents a shipping container that's located off to one side of a property and has a carpenter who uses it as a workshop for $300 per month.

Used shipping containers are cheap to buy and can be placed pretty much anywhere.

In multifamily buildings, you can charge for parking. It's an easy revenue generator.

Single-item storage can be an easy way to generate revenue, too, like space for someone's motor home, car, truck, trailer, boat, etc. The takeaway here is that if you have extra space, don't let it go to waste. Storage opportunities can be a great way to earn extra money.

Commercial Real Estate

I can remember the first time I had a meeting with my new accountant. He said he was located in the Hawthorne Business Centre but when I showed up, it was an old car dealership converted into several small offices. I was greeted by a receptionist in a grand entranceway and told her who I was looking for. She directed me to an office on the second floor.

The floor had about 10 offices, all different small businesses. When I inquired about the setup, he explained how he used to work from home but liked having an office closer to the city that allowed him to separate his work and family life. He also mentioned that it was an inexpensive alternative to renting traditional office space. It was a great setup too. Not only did he have a nice little secured office, but he also had a shared receptionist to collect packages, answer the phone, and take messages. The building was also equipped with a shared boardroom. As far as long-term tenants go—well, let's just say he's still working out of the same place over a decade later.

Even with the work-from-home movement, people will still need offices to hold meetings or collaborate with colleagues. While it's true that I pretty much used every type of online meeting forum during the pandemic, let's face it—nothing beats face to face. Even the banter, camaraderie and idea sharing gets filtered, censored, and minimized online. We are social beings, so providing an office space with private and group options can be a great real estate investing idea.

Now, before you run out and convert some old warehouse into a trendy office space for would-be work-from-home folks, you may want to follow the story of some of the people that went all in on this concept. One of the companies I'm referring to is called WeWork. Their story sort of rises, falls, and is back on the rise.[29]

Founded in 2010 by Adam Neumann and Miguel McKelvey, WeWork

is a coworking real estate company that has a head office located in New York. Right now, WeWork's office spaces are spread across 86 cities in 32 countries.

In 2014, WeWork's investors included the following:

- JP Morgan Chase & Co.

- Goldman Sachs

- Harvard Corporation

- Benchmark[30]

Yes, big names indeed. "Coworking" means the leveraging of common office infrastructure and facilities by several individual freelancers, start-ups, or companies. So, what coworking companies like WeWork do is lease properties from landlords and renovate them into a coworking space. They then sublease the coworking space to freelancers, start-ups, and companies.

The advantage of coworking for clients is lesser costs. Since the common infrastructure like printers, internet, cafeteria, kitchens, and restrooms are shared by many, the cost is lower when compared to leasing a full-fledged office facility.

This is just a segment of many in the commercial real estate investing space. Commercial real estate is a broad area that can consist of retail stores, strip malls, restaurants, office buildings, etc. It can be quite a bit more challenging to get financing for commercial real estate. However, the rewards of long-term tenants and much higher rents can make it worthwhile.

The risks are that it can take longer to get a commercial tenant in place and that the revenue is dependent on the tenant's business being successful enough to pay the rent. This is why lenders often scrutinize commercial deals. The first thing that's different from small residential deals when it comes to financing is that the lender will want to know the net operating cost and have an accurate picture of the net operating income (NOI).

This can be tricky to verify if the building is vacant or has a low-rent tenant. Also, if the business occupying the property is selling it because they're moving, it becomes a vacant possession. Even with the internet cutting into retail stores, commercial real estate will always be in demand—at least for the foreseeable future. I mean it would be tough to get a haircut or massage online, wouldn't it?

There are also some restaurants that focus on delivery only, so they don't require a dine-in restaurant and can set up their cooking equipment anywhere. A recent article by Michelle Cheng talks about how popular food-delivery icon DoorDash plans to open "so-called ghost kitchens— which are essentially restaurants without a storefront," and she states that "the facilities allow restaurants to expand their footprint in a low-cost and flexible way, without the costly real estate and labour required of customer-facing locations."[31]

A personal story of mine happened recently when my nine-year-old son wanted a "Mr. Beast Burger." I asked what he meant, and apparently, he follows a popular YouTube star named Mr. Beast. Well, Mr. Beast started up a burger restaurant. What makes it interesting is that the food is prepared in ghost kitchens rather than having physical, branded locations. We did a Google search, and sure enough, you could order a Mr. Beast Burger right off the Uber Eats menu. We ordered it in, and when it arrived, it was in full, logoed packaging. I started to think, Wow, what a brilliant idea.

Warehouse Space

A recent example of this type of transaction occurred right in my city of Halifax, Nova Scotia, in 2021. About 10 years before, a large furniture manufacturer decided to build furniture overseas. They had a large 200,000-square-foot warehouse. They put it up for sale, but due to the size and location (the back side of an industrial park), there were no takers.

They ended up finally selling it to a company that had plans to do great things with this warehouse that never came to fruition. It then changed hands to a car dealer named O'Regan Properties Limited. In 2021, a large online retail distribution company that I am sure you know (Amazon) came to town, seeking giant warehouse space. They ended up purchasing it in a multimillion-dollar deal. Amazon is now looking to establish a new warehouse and fulfillment centre at the site.[32]

Keep your eye out for good warehouse space. Even with the online shopping movement growing everywhere, many companies are buying shipping containers full of goods to import and distribute. The distribution business requires warehouses, and that has made owning large warehouse space very valuable.

Wholesaling

A few years back, I connected with an old friend and business-networking buddy. We talked about what each other was up to. He asked about challenges I faced in the property game. I mentioned it was all about having the time to find deals. He asked whether someone would be willing to pay a fee if he were able to find a deal and assign it to them. I said yes, absolutely. It's called "wholesaling." He was not familiar with the term, but he was excited about the idea and wanted to get started.

I suggested he give it a try and place an add on a local classified site. On the buying side, I had him start attending our group meetings so he could get to know some potential buyers. I don't think he went more than a few days before he got a lead on a house. It was an older lady looking to sell quick, but she didn't want to renovate or deal with what she perceived as a complicated process dealing with real estate agents and lawyers.

The key for you as the deal finder is to get an agreement in place that allows for you or the assignee to move forward with a deal. You need to be connected with buyers, too, since the seller will likely only give you a week or so to meet conditions. What my friend does now is he gets an agreement together and secures the deal. Then he promotes the deal to local investors for a fee. Depending on the complexity of the deal or what he needs to do to help complete it, he charges a fee of $3K to $5K. He never owns the property, just the idea. The fee is for putting in the effort to find deals, and as many investors know, the money is not always hard to find, but the deals are.

The fee can also be deal dependent too. So if you're looking at commercial, large multifamily, or million-dollar-plus transactions, the fee might be higher. A wholesaler can be fee or percentage based. A wholesaler will simply find a deal and share the lead for a price. When the deal is completed, the fee is paid. Generally, the fee will be paid directly by a lawyer as part of the deal disbursements. For me, I would gladly pay a fee to have a prenegotiated deal. It would make the process of finding deals so much easier.

THIRTY-FOUR

SYNDICATION, CROWDFUNDING, AND FRACTIONAL OWNERSHIP

WHEN YOU'RE *an* INVESTOR, IT IS POSSIBLE TO minimize risk while still reaping some of the rewards. To open your mind to some of the possibilities available, let's start with a few of the basics on what you can or cannot offer to the general public.

Accredited Investors

These are investors that are not protected or regulated on what they invest in. This is a great group, and if you know a few of them, they can invest in your projects without government oversight. This group is considered by most to be sophisticated enough to know the risks of the investment they're considering.

To be considered an accredited investor, you need to meet provincial criteria. In Ontario, you'll need to have a minimum net worth of one million dollars (can be joint with a spouse) or an annual net income (before taxes) of $200,000 per year ($300,000 joint with a spouse).[33] This can differ slightly between Canada and the U.S., so make sure to check with your local regulatory body. Also, if you're offering an investment opportunity to an accredited investor, the burden is on you to verify.

I can remember talking to my lawyer about group funding for real estate. He explained the process from a legal standpoint and assured me that if I were to go on Facebook and start taking random people's money, and the investment failed, there could be serious legal repercussions involved. This could involve the SEC (Securities and Exchange Commission) or a similar organization imposing fines and recommending criminal charges.

Now that I have instilled fear in all of you, here's the next step.

Syndication

Real estate syndication involves a group of investors who get together to purchase real estate. The head of the syndicate is referred to as the sponsor. They find, manage, renovate, and find investors for the group. The downside is that it's a regulated form of investment. That means you will either need to find accredited investors or provide a prospectus to the SEC and to your potential investors explaining the details of the investment opportunity you are offering.

This document will need to include the risk factors as well as any potential returns. It's designed so the average investor can get a good idea of what they're going to invest in. It also keeps the head of the syndicate focused on what they said they were going to invest in. If it states you will be buying multifamily buildings, the syndicate cannot take your money and purchase Bitcoin or something else. If it does, the investors can complain to the SEC and the syndicate will be investigated.

Syndication can be a great way to fundraise for real estate. However, it can be expensive to initially set up, so you will need to have a solid plan.

Crowdfunded Real Estate

This is an up-and-coming way to invest in real estate. The way a crowdfunded organization is set up can vary. Some are super simple, while others are much more complicated. In most instances, the process begins by setting up a website. Then you ask for contributions for an amount of money to own a share of a property. In many cases the minimums are quite low, so you could get a share for (at the time of writing this book) for as little as $1,500 to $2,500.

I do want to provide a word of caution if you're looking into this option as a share purchaser. Make sure you find out what your potential exit strategy would be and know all the details before handing out your money. A lot of people buy into the crowdfunded real estate schemes for the excitement and feeling of ownership. It's especially popular in areas with high property values. But it can be a very risky way to invest, and you have very little control over your investment. For this reason, it's also important to examine how the company selling you the shares makes money.

- ⊙ Do they collect a finder's fee for finding properties?

- ⊙ Do they own the real estate company buying and selling the property?

- ⊙ What do they charge for maintenance and property management fees?

- ⊙ Do they charge an annual fee to be part of the group?

If you Google crowdfunded real estate, you will quickly be overwhelmed with the number of options. One way you can check this information is to use Fundrise.com. According to their website, "with Fundrise, you can invest in a low-cost, diversified portfolio of institutional-quality real estate. [They] combine state-of-the-art technology with in-house expertise to reduce fees and maximize your long-term return potential."[34]

Fractional Ownership

This can be a great way to own a property, and it's generally set up more like a joint venture rather than a crowdfunded setup. The way fractional ownership works is a property is divided into shares. This includes the deed, so you own a portion of the property. This is more common with vacation-related properties, but this doesn't always mean you get to stay in the property.

A simple example would be for you to have land next to the ocean, and you decide you want to build a resort. You could sell turnkey villas using a fractional ownership model, then lease back the villa and rent it at a daily rate for your guests. The lease fee would go back to the fractional owners, and they would earn revenue based on their portion of the ownership minus an administration and maintenance fee.

This can be a win-win for both the resort owner and the investor. Often this type of arrangement would include deals for staying at the resort. Other types of fractional units are set up more like a time-share where you get to use the property for a designated time of the year. The great part about fractional ownership is that you can split basically anything with a deed into several owners. The options are almost limitless.

You'll want to understand the management fees charged to operate the fund, have a record of their activity, and have the ability to find good properties to lend mortgage funds to.

THIRTY – FIVE

BECOME A LENDER

TO BECOME A LENDER, YOU'LL *need* TO HAVE your own capital or have access to other sources of cash to lend out. In its simplest form, you could set up a joint venture structure, but after providing the financing, you will receive your money back with interest and the up-front fee (generally 10% of the loan). You can also provide money in the form of a simple mortgage if you're looking for a continuous return.

The key is to keep the money flowing. A person in my real estate group often posts smaller private-lending opportunities like the following example. (Obviously you would need more information.)

Investment opportunity:

- $17,000

- A $2,000 lender fee

- ⊙ An interest rate of 15%

- ⊙ A $1,000 broker fee

- ⊙ $13,000 to client

- ⊙ A required payment of $212.50 per month

- ⊙ A one-year minimum, possibly two

This type of smaller loan is usually for a renovation or part of a down payment. The terms are generally shorter as well.

THIRTY-SIX

PASSIVE INVESTMENTS

A REAL ESTATE INVESTMENT TRUST (REIT) *is* a financial investment that's traded on the stock market. The great part about a REIT is that 90% of the profits must legally go to the unit holders in the form of distributions, like dividend-paying stocks. (However, the payouts are not generated by the company's holdings.)[35] They also have limits on the amount of cash they can hold in reserve.

REITs have become very popular over the past few years,[36] but I will caution you to read the prospectus, that way you will understand what your money will be invested in. You can do a quick Google search and find hundreds to choose from. Most will have a class of real estate they invest in.

Some examples could include the following:

- ◉ Shopping malls or commercial retail

- ◉ Office buildings

- ◉ Industrial buildings

- ◉ Self-storage facilities

- ◉ Residential housing

- ◉ Mobile home parks

Many REITs are also into development, so they may also construct buildings prior to leasing them. Some may also focus on various types of buildings. It could be anything from low to high income.

CONCLUSION

IF YOU'VE CHOSEN *the* LIFESTYLE OF BEING A landlord or property manager, I hope you've found this book useful. Make sure you mark pages and keep it as a manual to help if you get into a situation that you're not sure about.

My wife and I are extremely passionate about the world of real estate investing and have met so many amazing tenants, realtors, other landlords, property managers, and contractors over the years that it makes for a rewarding lifestyle—but one that's not for everyone.

Though we often do see some big returns financially, the current gains are being reinvested into the properties. One of the biggest rewards is being able to provide great homes to great people.

It requires you to have thick skin, a pleasing personality, the patience of a saint, the willingness to work 24/7, the problem-solving skills of Einstein, and the ability to see the positive in every situation.

A good friend once told me there were no good or bad situations, just situations. I think my best advice to a new property manager or landlord is to surround yourself with like-minded individuals. Get educated, take a property management course, and join a real estate group. If there aren't any in your area, you can join online.

I hope you enjoyed this book. If you have any feedback, I would love to hear from you. You can reach me at landlordbydesign@gmail.com, on Twitter @michaelpcurrie, or through the following websites:

www.facebook.com/landlordbydesign

www.linkedin.com/company/landlord-by-design/

If you are seeking information on how to manage your properties, make sure to grab a copy of *Landlord by Design: Complete Guide to Residential Property Management.*

Thank you for reading my book.

ACKNOWLEDGEMENTS

THE FIRST SHOUT-OUT *goes* TO MY WIFE, SHELLY Currie. She's also my property management and landlord partner. It's so amazing that I was able to find someone to share my business and life with. We have two amazing boys, Hudson (14) and Wesley (10). I am so grateful to have my family on this awesome journey of life.

I want to shout out to our business partner and vice president of The Fort Nova Group (our real estate investment company), Michael Thibeau. I also want to thank my dad, Don Currie, and stepmother, Maureen Currie, who on more than one occasion have stepped in to help with various property management and cleaning jobs. Sometimes, we need all the help we can get to meet tight timelines.

In addition, to my family and close friends, I will say many business associates either introduced me to or directly helped me build the business, solved tenant issues, or played a supporting role in my success. You know who you are, and I thank you.

Of course, a special thanks to all my landlordbydesign.com subscribers, the folks who purchased and read my first book, *Landlord by Design:*

Complete Guide to Residential Property Management, and have read my blog over the years.

And finally, to all the landlords and real estate folks who shared and continue to share stories for not only this book but also my first book and blog.

You all mean so much to me.

GLOSSARY

Accountant: The term "accountant" is very broad and covers a lot of territory. It can be used to describe anyone from a bookkeeper to someone setting up offshore family trusts. They often keep track of and distribute the revenue coming in, monitor the expenses going out, and handle government forms, such as tax returns.

Cap rate: Cap rate = Net operating income divided by the purchase price

For example, you are looking to purchase a 10-unit property. The price is $800,000. The revenue it generates from rent, laundry, parking, and storage is $104,000 per year. The expenses (not including debt service) are $30,000 per year. The net operating income would be $74,000.

If we take $74,000 divided by $800,000, this equals a 9% cap rate (annual rate of return, not including debt service).

Capital expenditure: As it relates to a piece of real estate, this would be an item purchased that increases the usable life of the property and increases the value. It's the opposite of depreciation.

Cash call: Additional cash required for upgrades to a property over and above the initial purchase of the property or shares of the property. This is generally required when working capital is not available.

Cash flow: Cash flow is the amount of money left over after all expenses are paid. It can be broken down by month, quarter, or year. A basic example is as follows:

- Rent (revenue): $1,500

- Less expenses/mortgage: $800

- Insurance: $100

- Property tax: $200

- Water: $150

- Lawn care: $60

- Maintenance: $50

- Total expenses: $1,360

- Rent (revenue) $1,500 minus expenses $1,360 = a cash flow amount of $140 per month.

Class of buildings: Class A buildings are upscale. They compete for the higher-income tenants. They will have rents that are above the average for the area. An A-class building will also have the top-of-the-line appliances for the area, items like granite countertops and stainless steel appliances. Class B buildings are average. They compete for tenants looking for nice, clean rental space. A B-class building would be in a good neighbourhood. The rents would be at about average for the area. The finishes would likely be white instead of stainless steel. Class-C buildings are more functional or utilitarian. The units might be renovated but would have basic appliances and cupboards. The rents would be below the average. C-class buildings are found in lower-income areas.

Co-signer: The co-signer is a person who's liable for the terms and conditions of a lease but does not live in the rented space. A co-signer must meet all the qualifying requirements of the landlord. They would be necessary if a person (such as a student) might not meet income or rental history requirements to rent an apartment. They may also be necessary if an applicant does not meet credit rating requirements.

Customer service: Customer service has three main components: communication, attitude, and relationships. It's about listening and providing your customers (tenants) what they want.

Damage deposit: The damage deposit is an amount paid to the landlord when a lease is signed for any damages caused by the tenant. The damage deposit is kept in trust by the landlord for the duration of the lease. If the rented space does not have any damage after the tenant moves out, then it will be returned to the tenant. The amount you're allowed to collect (if any) is regulated by the local tenancy board. Another term for a damage deposit is "security deposit."

Debt-service ratio: The ratio between the amount of income you bring in versus the amount of the payments you're required to make on current debt obligations.

Deductible: A deductible is the portion of an insurance claim that the owner is responsible for. An example would be that if you had a sewer backup that cost $10,000 in damages and you had a $5,000 deductible, then the insurance company would pay the claim less the deductible. It would mean you get $5,000. The deductible can be adjusted. You can save money on insurance premiums by increasing your deductible, but you need to be prepared to bear the extra expense if you have a claim.

Default: Default describes when a tenant does not pay the rent. They are in default.

Depreciation: The reduction in the value of an asset over time. In residential real estate, buildings get old and worn out; therefore, the values of the buildings depreciate (become less over time).

Eviction: Eviction is the legal process by which a tenant may be removed from a property due to violations of the terms and conditions of the lease. Reasons for an eviction could be for not paying rent, for operating an illegal business (such as dealing drugs), or for being a danger to other tenants in the building. The eviction process is based on the tenancy laws of a specific area.

Giving notice: Giving notice is when a tenant lets you know they will be leaving. Every lease should include a specified time period for when a tenant has to let you know they intend to leave. Another term for this is "notice to quit."

Hard-money lender: An individual or organization that loans money at higher-than-average interest rates. Hard-money lenders are generally used for real estate deals that are considered too risky for a conventional bank. Terms are often based on interest-only payments and short terms. The loans are often used as a bridge until a property is renovated and has enough appraised value to be refinanced by a conventional bank and the hard money is paid back in full. They may also be referred to as an "alternative lender."

House hacking: When you live in a property and rent out a portion to cover some or all of your living expenses.

Landlord: A landlord is the property owner, the person or corporation that has all or partial ownership of a building.

Lawyer: A lawyer is the person who advises clients on legal matters. Items such as real estate transactions, wills, and joint venture contracts will need to be reviewed by a lawyer. In Canada, "lawyer" is a common term, used similarly to "attorney" in the U.S. In Canada, lawyers follow the rules of English common law (except for Quebec, which follows civil law).[37]

Lease: The lease is a signed agreement between the landlord and tenant. There are several kinds of leases. A lease agreement contains a series of terms and conditions that are agreeable to the landlord and tenant. Residential leases must be structured in a way to comply with local tenancy laws and regulations. Most government websites will have standard lease forms for residential leases. Commercial leases do not usually have many restrictions.

Lease up: The term "lease up" describes the process of getting signed leases in place on space that is available for rent.

Make ready: A "make ready" is the process of getting a space ready for rent. A make ready could include anything from cleaning to a full renovation. A typical make ready would be a paint job, cleaning, and basic maintenance repairs (like a sticky lock).

Occupancy date: The occupancy date is the date that the tenant's lease starts. On the occupancy date, the tenant will be required to have all required utilities hooked up in their name. The tenant is not required to move into the space on this date; however, the lease will begin.

Project manager: A project manager is a person or company that oversees a specific renovation. The project manager will generally work under the guidance of the property manager or landlord. An example would be if you were going to renovate or build something, the project manager would arrange the tradespeople required, such as a general contractor, electrician, and plumber. The project manager will keep a close watch on the progress of the work and make sure the project runs smoothly. In many cases, a property manager may also offer the services of a project manager.

Property manager: The property manager is the individual or company that takes care of the daily operations of a property. They will also do or oversee activities such as making sure all spaces are cleaned and rented and that maintenance and repairs are taken care of. The property manager works for the landlord, or in a small operation, it can be the same person.

Real estate investment trusts (REITs): Publicly traded companies allow individual investors to buy shares in real estate portfolios that receive income from a variety of properties.

Redemption period: This is the designated period after a tax sale property has been purchased that allows the owner to pay the tax in full and reclaim the property. It's usually a period of six months.

Rental income: Rental income is the amount of money you claim on your tax returns that you've collected from your rental properties. It's important to make sure you get proper tax advice and work with an accountant who's familiar with doing tax accounting for landlords. There are several tax benefits (in the form of expenses) to owning rental properties.

Renters' beige: Renters' beige is a paint colour that can be used to paint all rented spaces. It's a nonoffensive colour that appeals to most people. It can be manufactured by most paint companies, and the specific shade is not important as long as it is not too dark or too light. It should be purchased in a five-gallon bucket to maximize savings and allow you to always have enough on hand to paint a few units. Top-quality paint is recommended to maximize coverage and cover imperfections in walls.

Revenue: Revenue is the gross amount of money you collect from your tenants. When you collect rent, it's considered revenue. It's the amount before expenses are deducted. A building could have a lot of revenue but could have a very low or negative net income, once you deduct the expenses.

Security deposit: See "damage deposit."

Squatter: A squatter is a person or persons who reside in a space but don't sign a lease or pay rent. It's more common to find squatters in abandoned buildings; however, they have been noted to show up in vacant spaces that are available for paying tenants. Some areas have rights for squatters, and you may have to follow an eviction process to get rid of them.

Tax sale: A tax sale is when a municipality, city, parish, town, or village puts a property up for auction to get the taxes owed on the property paid up to date.

Tenant: The tenant is the person or company that occupies a rented space. They're the customer of the landlord or property manager.

Turnover: Turnover refers to when one tenant leaves and a new one moves in. It can be the most expensive part of owning rental properties.

Types of paint jobs: A deluxe paint job is where the baseboards, trim, and ceiling are all painted white, and the walls are a different colour. A basic paint job is where the ceiling is white, and the trim and baseboards are the same colour as the walls. A quick and dirty paint job is where the ceiling, walls, trim, and baseboards are all one colour.

Vacancy: Vacancy refers to unoccupied space that's available for rent.

Vacancy rate: The vacancy rate is the estimated amount of unoccupied rented space in a particular area. If an area has a vacancy rate of 10%, then you could count on one in every 10 units being vacant. It is important to monitor your building's vacancy rate to the area's vacancy rate. The vacancy rate in most established areas is usually between 1% and 6%. Greater than 6% usually indicates an area with a low population, too much rental supply, a depressed economy, or a combination of several factors.

Wholesaler: A wholesaler can be fee based or percentage based. A wholesaler finds a deal and shares the deal for a fee. When the deal is completed, the fee is paid. Generally, the fee will be paid directly by a lawyer as part of the deal disbursements.

ABOUT THE AUTHOR

MICHAEL **C**URRIE *is* **A LANDLORD,** property manager, author, and owner of the company Landlord by Design. Based in Canada, Michael got his start in the early 2000s as an investor flipping houses, and by the end of 2009, he was using a buy and hold strategy with his investments. As a member of the IPOANS (Investment Property Owners of Nova Scotia) organization, Michael further gained extensive experience with property managers, tenants, tradespeople, contractors, and more.

After discovering a need for property management education, Michael started the Landlord by Design blog in 2015 to offer guidance and share his expertise. While it began as part-therapy, part-record keeping, Michael soon realized that many readers wanted to learn how to participate in real estate investing in addition to property management.

Michael published his first book, Landlord by Design: Complete Guide to Residential Property Management, in 2016. This effort was the result of trial and error while working with various investment strategies from tax sales and student properties to zero-money-down investing

Michael lives in Nova Scotia, Canada, with his wife, Shelly, and their two children. When he isn't writing about real estate, Michael can be found spending time with his family, volunteering with his favourite nonprofit organizations, or enjoying the social clubs of Halifax. Learn more at www.landlordbydesign.com.

ENDNOTES

1   Louise DeNicola, "What Factors Affect Your Credit Score?," Credit Karma, updated January 20, 2022, https://www.creditkarma.com/advice/i/what-affects-your-credit-scores#somewhat-important-length-of-credit-history.

2   "How Government Bond Yields Relate to Mortgage Rates," True North Mortgage, updated November 2021, https://www.truenorthmortgage.ca/blog/how-government-bond-yields-relate-to-mortgage-rates.

3   "How Government Bond Yields Relate to Mortgage Rates."

4   "How Government Bond Yields Relate to Mortgage Rates."

5   "How Government Bond Yields Relate to Mortgage Rates."

6   Julie Broad, More Than Cashflow: The Real Risks & Rewards of Real Estate Investing (Los Angeles: Stick Horse Publishing, 2013), 165.

7   "Down Payments: 5% VS 20%," Centum, accessed February 21, 2022, https://www.centum.ca/Blog/Down-Payments-5-vs-20.

8   Ken Clark, "Recourse Loans vs. Non-Recourse Loan: Knowing the Difference," Investopedia, updated July 31, 2021, https://www.investopedia.com/ask/answers/08/nonrecourse-loan-vs-recourse-loan.asp.

9   Robert Stammers, "Top Things That Determine a Home's Value," Investopedia, updated July 30, 2021, https://www.investopedia.com/articles/mortgages-real-estate/08/housing-appreciation.asp.

10 "How Long Should I Keep Records?," Internal Revenue Service, updated August 5, 2021, https://www.irs.gov/businesses/small-businesses-self-employed/how-long-should-i-keep-records.

11 "How Long Should You Keep Your Income Tax Records?," Government of Canada, January 18, 2022, https://www.canada.ca/en/revenue-agency/services/tax/individuals/topics/about-your-tax-return/long-should-you-keep-your-income-tax-records.html.

12 Yvonne Colbert, "There's $97M Waiting for Homeowners with Kitec Plumbing. Why Don't They Claim It?," CBC News, January 10, 2019, https://www.cbc.ca/news/canada/nova-scotia/class-action-settlement-kitec-plumbing-1.4971290.

13 Colbert, "There's $97M Waiting for Homeowners."

14 Colbert, "There's $97M Waiting for Homeowners."

15 Mike Reynolds, "Radon Levels by State & Province – Why a Radon Test Is Essential," EcoHome, updated July 28, 2021, https://www.ecohome.net/guides/3520/radon-gas-levels-by-state-province-map-test-homes-basements-crawlspace/.

16 Spencer Rascoff, "Confirmed: Starbucks Knows the Next Hot Neighborhood Before Everybody Else Does," Quartz, January 28, 2015, https://qz.com/334269/what-starbucks-has-done-to-american-home-values/.

17 "Report on Housing Needs of Seniors," Government of Canada, 2017, https://www.canada.ca/en/employment-social-development/corporate/seniors/forum/report-seniors-housing-needs.html.

18 Susan Stobert and Kelly Cranswick, "Looking after Seniors: Who Does What for Whom?," Canadian Social Trends (Autumn 2004), https://www150.statcan.gc.ca/n1/en/pub/11-008-x/2004002/article/7002-eng.pdf?st=zafHy90F.

19 Sunil Tulsiani and Brian Tracy, The Secret to Wealth: And Secrets from the World's Top Leaders (Brampton, Canada: Private Investment Club, 2018).

20 Lisa Rennie, "How to Avoid CMHC Fees," Loans Canada, updated July 6, 2021, https://loanscanada.ca/mortgage/avoid-cmhc-fees/.

21 Rebecca Aydin, "How 3 Guys Turned Renting Air Mattresses in Their Apartment into a $31 Billion Company, Airbnb," Insider, updated September 20, 2019, https://www.businessinsider.com/how-airbnb-was-founded-a-visual-history-2016-2.

22 "Quarantine or Isolation," Government of Canada, updated February 18, 2022, https://travel.gc.ca/travel-covid/travel-restrictions/isolation.

23 Jayden Jhutti, "AirB-N-Quarantine? Metro Vancouver Rooms Being Rented Out for Isolating Travelers," CityNews, updated May 14, 2021, https://vancouver.citynews.ca/2021/05/14/metro-vancouver-quarantine-rental/.

24 "Rental Vacancy Rate," IBISWorld, updated January 26, 2022, https://www.ibisworld.com/ca/bed/rental-vacancy-rate/15065/.

25 "Rooming House Licensing By-law Review," Ottawa, updated February 8, 2018, https://ottawa.ca/en/city-hall/public-engagement/projects/rooming-house-licensing-law-review#definition-rooming-house-.

26 "We Are a Social Purpose Organization," Happipad, accessed February 21, 2022, https://happipad.com/social-purpose/.

27 "An Expert Guide to Joint Ventures in Real Estate," We Lend, March 20, 2021, https://www.welendllc.com/blog/joint-ventures-real-estate-guide.

28 "Rent-to-Own Homes in Canada 2022," WOWA, accessed February 22, 2022, https://wowa.ca/rent-to-own-homes.

29 Leticia Miranda, "WeWork Imploded in 2019. The Pandemic Brought It Back to Life," NBC News, May 24, 2021, https://www.nbcnews.com/business/business-news/wework-imploded-2019-pandemic-brought-it-back-life-n1267957.

30 Vishal Gupta, "Why Is WeWork Failing (Case Study)," Bizain, June 2, 2021, https://www.bizain.com/wework-failure/.

31 Michelle Cheng, "DoorDash Isn't Just Delivering Meals—It's Making Them Too," Quartz, July 29, 2021, https://qz.com/2039684/doordash-is-launching-ghost-kitchens-to-make-food-for-restaurants/.

32 Noushin Ziafati, "Amazon Sets Up Shop in Dartmouth Business Park," Saltwire, April 20, 2021, https://www.saltwire.com/atlantic-canada/business/amazon-sets-up-shop-in-halifax-regional-municipality-100577768/.

33 "Accredited Investor," Accredited Capital Corporation, accessed February 21, 2022, https://accreditedcapitalcorp.com/cadosc45.php.

34 "Welcome to the Future of Real Estate Investing," Fundrise, accessed February 21, 2022, https://fundrise.com.

35 Sam Bourgi, "In Spite of the 90% Rule, Why Do Some REITs Have Poor Payout Ratios?," Dividend.com. accessed February 21, 2022, https://www.dividend.com/how-to-invest/in-spite-of-90-rule-why-do-some-reits-have-poor-payout-ratios/.

36 "What's a REIT?," Nareit, accessed February 21, 2022, https://www.reit.com/what-reit/history-reits.

37 "Where Our Legal System Comes From," Government of Canada, January 9, 2021, https://www.justice.gc.ca/eng/csj-sjc/just/03.html.

www.ingramcontent.com/pod-product-compliance
Lightning Source LLC
Chambersburg PA
CBHW022130050726
47590CB00002B/495